Teach Me To Fly

Teach Me To Fly

INSIGHTS INTO EARLY CHILDHOOD NEO-HUMANIST EDUCATION

By Nancy "Niiti" Gannon

InnerWorld Publications
San Germán, Puerto Rico
www.innerworldpublications.com

All Rights reserved by the author. No part of this book may be reproduced or transmitted in any form or by any means, electronic or mechanical, including photocopying, recording, or by any information storage or retrieval system, without permission in writing from the publisher, except for the inclusion of brief quotations in a review.

First edition © 1999
Second Edition © 2018

The last chapter, "Yoga in Schools," was written by MJ Glassman

Chief editors: Paula "Parvati" Brinkley and Helen (Vimala) Wells.

Layout and cover design: Devashish Donald Acosta

ISBN: 9781881717645

Library of Congress Control Number: 2018941368

CONTENTS

Introduction — Sarkar, Renaissance Man	1
Neo-Humanism, A New Social Philosophy	5
The Call of the Hour	10
The Educator As Guru	14
Precious Is The Child	25
The Awakening Of Spirit	36
Universal Love	42
Never Can Get Enough Of Morality	51
Tears And Smiles Of Emotional Growth	62
Can I Play With You?	69
Becoming a Guiding Star	80
What I Want To Know Is?	89
Writing Is As Natural As Holding A Spoon	103
I Believe I Can Fly	110
In That Special Place	118
Putting It All Together	123
Yoga In Schools	126

INTRODUCTION — SARKAR, RENAISSANCE MAN

Prabhat Rainjan Sarkar (1921 to 1990), is the originator of Neo-humanist Education. This book explains his major educational ideas and adapts them to early childhood education. Before understanding his educational philosophy, it is helpful to become acquainted with the founder. Who was Sarkar? He was a Renaissance man. In a simple life span he completed an extensive array of achievements. While building a global spiritual and service organization called Ananda Marga, he left a legacy of over three hundred volumes of literature on various disciplines including education, spirituality, linguistics, psychology, history, and politics. His works are not only great in their own right, but they also "ignite the fire" in others.

Particularly in the field of education, Sarkar directed growth in educational theory and practice by guiding his volunteers and instructing them to open more than seven hundred schools throughout the world. From the early 1960's, he had a radical new vision of how to educate young children. On February 21, 1982, by introducing the philosophy of Neo-humanism through a series of discourses, he more concretely solidified his model of education. Neo-humanism blended Sarkar's previous ideas on Universalism, spirituality, morality, and science to form a new social outlook. He extended the spirit of Humanism to include love for animals, plants, and inanimate objects. For example, he started a global plant exchange program to save and propagate thousands of plants species around the world. Neo-humanism joined the educational field to the field of ecology and environmental awareness.

This book attempts to help a novice understand education in the light of Neo-humanism and other inspirational guidance that Sarkar provided. As the education field in general covers many ages and aspects, this book confides itself to early childhood education, from birth to eight years old. It is widely known that these ages belong to the most critically formative period, unduplicated again during life. That is precisely why Sarkar looked at the formative period as advantageous for the introduction of Neo-humanism to youngsters. Sarkar said:

> "Some people may ask - why do you run Kindergarten schools and not High Schools, Degree Colleges and Universities? A Kindergarten school is something basic and the mission of man making is accomplished here. If one has already become a thief or a dacoit (criminal), in that case, the university education for such a person is of no avail. One is molded in one's childhood. If one received fundamentals of education in the formative period of life, one will keep oneself all right in the teeth of the heaviest odds in life. A bamboo, when green, can be shaped or bent in any way you like. Once it ripens, any attempt to reshape it will break it. That's why, more stress is to be laid on Kindergarten schools. That is the first phase of man-making."[1]

From birth to first grade children develop their character and belief systems for life. It takes tremendous effort after this period to change them significantly. Today with more daycares, nurseries, and preschools caring for the young, education increasingly takes on an importance similar to that of the family in the role of molding children. With non-family members caring for young children, it is important that these caregivers perceive themselves as an extension of the family so that their young charges will receive tender care.

Although this book will only highlight and expand Sarkar's educational ideas, it is important to mention that Sarkar's accomplishments in other areas directly and indirectly influence his work in education. In the field of philology and linguistics, Sarkar wrote volumes about the Bengali and Sanskrit languages, books that will require years of scholarly study to be fully understood. These volumes trace the evolution of words, phrases, and cultural traditions of Indian languages, and give new and important insights to Indo-European and other languages of the world.

In the field of science, Sarkar introduced the theory of Microvita in 1986. Through a series of discourses, Sarkar struck at the heart of conventional physics and biology, as he pointed out that the basic building blocks of life are Microvita — emanations of pure consciousness. The Microvita theory provides the link between the worlds of perception and conception; thus it implies that the distinct disciplines of physics, biology, and mathematics will merge into one science of understanding the real nature of the universe.

In the field of music, literature, and arts, Sarkar urged artists to do art for service and blessedness and not "art for art's sake". He also gave guidelines to accomplish these goals. Sarkar not only wrote long philosophical theses; he enriched literature with children's stories, fiction, comedy, and drama.

One of his significant artistic contributions is the five thousand and eighteen songs known as Prabhat Sam'giit (Songs of a New Dawn), which he started giving in 1982 until his death in 1990. These beautiful songs express the universality of the human heart. Most songs were written in Sarkar's mother tongue, Bengali. Bengali scholars have given the highest praise to these songs, in terms of their poetic and symbolic expressions.

Regarding the collective welfare of the society, Sarkar propounded the theory of PROUT (Progressive Utilization Theory). His theory explains the importance of maximum utilization and rational distribution of global resources and potentialities through the creation of a new social order. Also, an academic publisher has just launched a new university textbook that highlights the contribution that Sarkar made to the study of history. The book, *Macrohistory and Macrohistorians* (Praeger Publisher, 1997), is edited by Sohail Inyatullah and Johan Galtung. Johan Galtung, professor of Peace Studies and a winner of the " Right Livelihood Award" has said, "Sarkar will probably stand out as one of the truly great in this century, so much deeper and more imaginative than most."

As a Renaissance Man, Sarkar leads humanity in many exciting directions. In education his ideas profoundly change the way educators view their responsibilities, values, goals for children, and the process of learning. Before his death, he tirelessly gave a blueprint for a university complex called "Gurukul" that is being built in India today. It was the crown of his work in education. The following chapters explain his ideas and guidelines regarding education of young children.

NEO-HUMANISM, A NEW SOCIAL PHILOSOPHY

Men and women who value and care for the multitude
Stand out as rare flowers in the divine bouquet.
As dearly as they love others,
As preciously they feel the universe holding them.

Before discussing Neo-humanist education at length, first there has to be an understanding of the philosophy of Neo-humanism. What is the definition of Neo-humanism, and what are its salient concepts? Why was Neo-humanism needed at this juncture of human social development? The first chapter explains the philosophy of Neo-humanism. The remainder of the book will practically apply it to the field of education.

THE NEED FOR A NEW SOCIAL PHILOSOPHY

Today people want answers to the difficult and growing social problems. There is a need for an immediate stop to global suffering and stress. To increase human happiness and well being, concrete solutions must be created. Generally, all solutions begin in the arena of ideas. Unfortunately, in the realm of ideas, scientific thought leaps ahead and social ideas lag behind. In the social sphere, fewer ideas have appeared that can successfully move the world forward. Few ideas emerge because clarity is lacking in the social field. There are two explanations why people are equivocal and unclear. One is that many feel overwhelmed with the huge amount of problems to be sorted out; the other is that some individuals intentionally throw up smoke screens to keep people confused.

The roots of today's social issues are greed and selfishness. Rapid acceleration of avarice and self-interest causes people to exploit each other as well as their resources. For instance, half of the rainforests have vanished, mostly due to social mis-utilization. Every year ranchers cut down two and a half million hectares of rainforest in the Amazon region and Central America primarily in order to graze and feed cattle. Eventually, most of the cattle ends up as meat that is exported to the United States for fast food hamburgers.[2] Former United Nations Secretary General Kurt Waldheim has said that the food habits of the rich countries are the key cause of global hunger. The United Nations strongly recommends that rich countries cut down on their meat consumption.[3] Greed and selfishness are hindering the world's well-rounded development.

Society needs to establish new social ideas that will enable people to form positive human and environmental relationships. A new philosophy that adapts to the changing contours of society while it widens mankind's vision is necessary. In the past all philosophies failed to meet these expectations. Some philosophies were overly spiritual, lacking rationality. Others pertained to the physical realm, but could not balance the hard realities of the world or inspire the finer aspects of humanity.[4]

Without a proper philosophy, social leaders cannot properly proceed and guide others. For instance, Mary is a university professor who teaches educational philosophy to future teachers. She believes that the difference between ordinary and extraordinary teachers depends on their values, inspiration, and vision. Some students, Mary found, do not grasp how important philosophy and guiding values and concepts are. Instead they overly rely on economic incentives, general educational understanding, and the love of children to motivate them. Her students that do appreciate philosophy and higher values tend to be eclectic, adopting aspects from various philosophies. Although this approach broadens, ideas if not well thought out frequently fail to gel together into a cohesive and clear whole.

The social arena requires strong ideas that motivate people to form positive human and environmental relationships. Ideas well rooted in practical application while spurring progressive and higher visions. New concepts to remove selfishness and greed while offering greater fulfillment.

ADVENT OF NEO-HUMANISM

In 1982 Sarkar propounded Neo-humanism as the social philosophy that provides new direction and answers to the global crisis. Neo-humanism, although it clearly has practical implications, does not fail to cultivate the all around needs of humanity. Human life consists of physical, mental, and spiritual aspects, so the philosophy must protect and develop these. Recognizing the basic realities of this world, Neo-humanism acts differently from other philosophies. Primarily, it comprehends the full diversity of human nature and embraces it. While understanding the array of human characteristics, Neo-humanism does not miss what remains at the heart of human expression. Neo-humanism identifies humanity's most precious treasure. After surveying the panorama of human existence, the expression of love remains as humanity's most precious achievement. When commenting on love, Sarkar explains,

> "Because it is such a tender inner asset, to preserve it from the onslaughts of materialism, one must build a protective fence around it, just as people put up a guard-rail around a small tender plant. Now the question is what is this protective fence? It is a proper philosophy that will establish the correct harmony between the spiritual and material worlds, and be a perennial source of inspiration for the onward movement of society."[5]

Until recently, people heralded humanists as those with the most ideal social outlook, for humanists look upon all people as inherently equal, good, and productive with tremendous potential to create. Humanists have concern for peoples' welfare regardless of sex, creed, race, or nationality; yet, humanists do not address the rights and needs of other creatures. A humanist need not care for the plight of ecology, and may thoughtlessly inflict cruelty on animals.

Neo-humanism blends a greater array of ideas such as Universalism, spirituality, morality, and science to form a new social outlook, a new theory of universal humanity that embraces all forms of existence. Neo-humanism stretches the imagination and hearts' compassion to the fullest. Incorporating spirituality, it includes the oneness of life, an idea that everything is a manifestation of Infinite Consciousness. Neo-humanism believes that behind this vast universe there exists one, loving, and Universal Consciousness, connecting all individual entities. When people understand that everything depicts the One, Infinite Consciousness, they want to extend loving kindness towards others. Neo-humanism expands the humanists' love for humanity to include other entities — animals, plants, and inanimate objects.

Neo-humanism understands how sweet is the treasure of love that people feel towards their children, partners, and friends. This same love tenderly appears in different relationships. In its highest form it transforms into devotional or spiritual love. At its pinnacle, love broadens the mind and heart from a limited view to a limitless one, a three hundred and sixty-degree view that encompasses the myriad forms of creation. This outlook changes people and their relationships. Writer Anne De Lenclos wrote of this spirit of transformation:

> "Today a new sun rises for me; everything lives, everything is animated, everything seems to speaks to me of my passion, everything invites me to cherish it."[6]

Another expression or term for Neo-humanism is "Universal Humanism". It extends human love to all beings, and acknowledges the rights of other species. Such a concept radically and humbly stops people from acting as masters of the planet. Rather this concept turns humanity into global caretakers. "Universal Humanism" envisions each being as essential to the cosmos. When people look up at a starry night sky and realize their human smallness amongst such bright magnitude, they gain insight of their own and others' splendor. They realize each being shines with existential glory. Moreover, each one's value is beyond the realm of human conception, and one can only guess at it.

THE CALL OF THE HOUR

A child absorbs herself in picking a gardenia
flower off a low branch.
Quickly she turns to a nearby teacher and offers it
without hesitation.
Beauty catches the innocent mind and then a whim
inspires her to pass it.

Sarkar introduced Neo-humanism to awaken new beauty and benevolence in the mental world. Neo-humanism appreciates beauty in everything. It brings truth, harmony, and new charm to the world and can suit the poet, the physicist, and the educator. Education carries the most significant role in the spread of Neo-humanism. Although every field has importance, initially education takes priority. It is through education that changes in the mental arenas occur on a large social scale.

EDUCATION IN CRISIS

Education's purpose is to generate and provoke an atmosphere for new mental and spiritual growth. Unfortunately, education has fallen to maintaining the status quo under the control of individuals with hidden interests. The love of power prompts leaders to sacrifice education to secretive interests. Truly, education must develop a mature mind in individuals who will lead society towards a greater goal. With proper guidance and movement, the children spiral to higher levels than their predecessors. When education becomes a victim of power, the educational standard drops and children's development suffers acutely.

Similar to education, family life also becomes a pawn in power plays by outside groups. In developed countries families move frequently for jobs, and extended families have difficulty keeping together and supporting each other. Parenting turns into an isolated endeavor. For instance, when Bill was a child he grew up with weekly family gatherings where fourteen cousins played together while six aunts chatted around the table and four uncles played pinochle. Grandpa sat in the chair watching everyone and Grandma fussed in the kitchen. Over time the family changed and moved, leaving only two cousins and one aunt nearby. The rest relocated to other cities. Bill's children have bonded closely with only a few relatives, and they look upon the larger clan as distant figures in their life.

Big business further disrupts the healthy fabric of family life by subjecting the members to excessive materialism. Even children as young as preschool age are familiar with name brands and pester their parents for fast food items. Every age is bombarded with clever advertisements for goods. For instance, advertisements about super fighters can be either about laundry detergents or dolls. In general, the media carries the message that wealth and power measure success. Families find little or no support for ethical and spiritual enrichment. Consequently, in this atmosphere, both the family and the school often fail to properly cushion and support a child's growth.

Directly responsible for the family and school's plight is the increased power of big industry to control the lives of people. Multi-national corporations influence people's lives more than governments. How do they intentionally effect the material and social trends around the world? The annual sales income of multi-national corporations is greater than the gross national product of many countries. For example, the income of General Motors is larger than Switzerland, Pakistan, or South Africa. The average growth rate of successful global corporations is at two to three times that of the growth rate of most developed countries, including the United States. Daily decisions in firms like GM, Microsoft, Shell, Exxon, and others have tremendous impact. The multi-national corporations' powers lie in controlling the creation of wealth worldwide. They determine where people live, what work they do, and what they eat. Indirectly, through their grants, multi-national corporations effect what information schools will teach, thus influencing what kind of society the future generation will inherit. Theirs is not a blind force; it is well thought out and pre-planned.

Education has to be free of multi-national corporations' clutches, so it may test out many ideas and strategies. Education stands at the forefront as the means to lead social conscience. With free rein and noble concepts to guide its process, education can eradicate the suffering that grips society. Only uplifting and sound principles can fully advance education in the right direction. Otherwise, education becomes more of a passport for privilege and prestige than a responsibility to serve others. Education must represent, not individual success and prominence, but the full expansion of human potentialities. Education must lead to an evolution of a compassionate outlook. If education merely stands for the accumulation of knowledge for its own sake, schooling leads to selfishness and intellectualism that slow the overall benefits for society. As Sarkar states, "They are 'educated' who have learned much, remembered much, and made use of their knowledge in everyday life. Their virtues I will call education."[7]

By applying Neo-humanistic ideas to education, Sarkar redefines the boundaries of education. Education for young children becomes a concerted effort to awaken in children universal love and social conscience so that they grow into people who care to improve the world. It translates into an emphasis on the whole child - physical, mental, and spiritual - with a sense of responsibility to all others.

All the key concepts of Neo-humanism alter the process of education. More than merely being theoretical concepts that influence education, they call for methods and curriculum different from those used in other systems. In the following chapters, the major components of Neo-humanism will unfold to give a clearer idea of the educational process.

THE EDUCATOR AS GURU

Eagerly a young child runs to pick a flower for her teacher.
Smiling, the teacher receives the gift and thanks the child.
In this simple gesture, they re-enact and exchange a sacred offering.

Teachers sit at the hub of the education process. What teachers believe and do not believe; what they do and do not do; and what they say and do not say makes up the learning experience. If educators venture to create a Neo-humanistic atmosphere, where every person, every being, is precious, they have made a very different commitment than doing work merely as a job for paychecks.

Sometimes people think the main work of a teacher consists of curriculum instruction. An educator's work involves many important aspects. One is the daily interaction and growth derived from play. Also, the spontaneous learning events, where children get excitedly carried away, are an important part of teaching. Equally valuable are moments of personal breakthroughs when a child reaches a deeper level of communication. The teacher encourages this deeper level of communication by not avoiding and hindering the child's expression of problems at home or school. Good educators follow the saying: "Let's talk. Let's all talk. What we don't talk about hurts us all."

TEACHERS' QUALIFICATIONS

Although teachers form the nucleus of education, most education theories generally do not fully outline the qualifications of teachers. Many theorists such as Vygotsky and Human Potential theorists view teachers as essential yet do not go into detail about who or what characteristics makes good teachers. Sarkar, more than any other, realized the importance of teachers and recognized the teacher's character as paramount. Sarkar understood that not everyone qualifies to become an educator, especially in the light of Neo-humanism. In Neo-humanism, it is not enough to subscribe to great ideals. These principles have to be embodied and become part of the character of the individual. Neo-humanist teachers have to live a Neo-humanistic life. Their efforts to introduce children to Neo-humanism come from within and from their personal example. A teacher, using a modern proverb, "has to walk the talk." Sarkar states,

> "Those who have acquired academic qualifications do not have an automatic right to become teachers. Teachers must possess such qualities as integrity, strength of character, righteousness, a sense of social service, unselfishness, an inspiring personality, and leadership capacity."[8]

Looking at each of the particular character qualities Sarkar required in Neo-humanist teachers gives insight into Neo-humanist education. With teachers of this caliber, children have an ideal model to imitate.

CHARACTER QUALITIES OF GOOD TEACHERS

INTEGRITY

Children learn mostly by example and watch every action of their teachers, even the ones a teacher does not want them to see. Children see who the teacher is on the inside and outside. Children perceive even if they cannot articulate what they see. When teachers engage in becoming ideal Neo-humanists by their thoughts and actions, they exhibit moral courage. This continuous effort to live and think in an ethical manner gains children's full trust, opens their hearts, and induces them to mimic. Through educators' good example, the children learn more about becoming ideal persons.

STRENGTH OF CHARACTER

There comes a time when all teachers are tested. Young children, especially children who have dysfunctional family backgrounds, know how to push buttons! Regardless of how noble and calm teachers are some children will trigger them. At the worst moments, the teacher who can dig in for a little more patience and love really has an opportunity to turn the tide. Only through a strong inner conviction is this possible. A weak person will not be able to maintain ideals in all interactions. When difficult children seek in negative ways for the teacher's attention or test to see how far they can go before the teacher will stop caring, the interaction will be unpleasant and emotions will rise to the surface. To give love at such a moment means a great deal to the child, but becomes very strenuous for the teacher. Only an educator of strong integrity can maintain affection and patience in stressful times. When a teacher shows integrity to troubled children not only do the children improve, but also all children benefit from the teacher's example. It gives new comfort and security to all the children under the teacher's care, and promotes a belief in others. Everyone advances in this situation, yet showing integrity to a difficult child is a test of fire and belongs to the strong hearted.

Teachers develop strength of character through a commitment to spiritual practices, a commitment to a process of self-development, and through the belief in noble ideas. The belief in universal love allows teachers to tap the perennial source of inspiration like a fountain that never dries. Any lesser outlook and belief will leave a teacher feeling empty and weak during stressful moments. Additionally, there are guidance skills and behavioral management information to help deal with difficult children. Strength of character results from an ongoing effort.

RIGHTEOUSNESS

Righteousness is doing right and being proper to others. Teachers, who work regularly with young children, gain first hand knowledge of the results of good or harmful care. Neohumanist teachers become "on fire" for the rights of children. They know humans have the potential to do right to each other if they apply themselves. It becomes increasingly hard to tolerate indifference by others and the society in general towards the plight and welfare of little children. Wisely, teachers look for similar minded company such as colleagues and parents to join up with and to work with for social change. Educators especially seek out good parents to enlist as their partners in helping children. A motivated parent can change a whole education system. Righteousness has good company and, similar to dry grass, it catches fire and spreads easily. Teachers must have a strong sense of righteousness.

SENSE OF SOCIAL SERVICE

An educator receives a wage but never gets properly compensated for their work and responsibility. Teaching includes love, care, patience, untiring effort, and inspiration. People who gravitate to this field need a sense of social service. They understand that giving to others exists for its sake, because it is noble and spiritual to do so. The reward comes in the form of the pleasant and satisfying feelings that arise in all the little breakthroughs and successes they see on a daily basis with their children. Teachers live the life of an apple tree. To the hungry, they offer fruits. With strong branches, they shade and protect. And the children that sit under their boughs receive the same patient care. Education is a giving profession, one for the service-minded.

UNSELFISHNESS

One-step more in Neo-humanism than the sense of social service consists of unselfishness or selfless service. Although it has similarities with service, it further describes attributes such as generosity and kindness that come to people who perform service for the right reasons. Although the teaching profession generally attracts service-minded persons, some teachers enter the profession for the wrong reasons. Service does not have to be selfless, for it can, unfortunately, come from the desire to gain name or fame. Salary and social security often pull people to service type professions.

Another reason people are attracted to service fields comes from hidden subconscious pulls formed in childhood. Many service professions fulfill personal drives to be over-responsible or to care for others as an escape from looking at their own needs. In some cases, for instance, being helpful was the only way in childhood that some children received attention. Overtime seeking approval by being helpful, becomes their habit and as adults draws them into service professions. For instance, Jerald was the elder son in a large family. His father was an alcoholic and sometimes physically struck his wife. As Jerald aged, he took responsibility to fix things at home and even intervened when his father became abusive. Gratefully, his mother praised him, increasingly relying upon his support. The stressful family situation, though, caused his parents to give him little unconditional appreciation. As an adult he became a conscientious teacher, often volunteering for extra programs. Unfortunately, he did not feel satisfaction for his effort. No matter how hard Jerald worked he felt incomplete. Such adults help from a subconscious unfulfilled need rather than an altruistic effort. In these cases, after serving they still feel a sense of emptiness rather than fulfillment. Therefore, service alone does not indicate the deeper and right qualifications a teacher needs. It requires selflessness, and this quality is the result of serving from a position of wholeness. Selflessness arises in a teacher who enjoys a higher level of personal maturity and teaches with the right reasons, truly for others. When selflessness occurs, one receives grace. Such individuals tap a spiritual flow or quality that softens their hearts towards others. Many individuals have to introspect and determine if they can find true generosity and kindness inside. It cannot be faked. It comes from grace and from being genuine.

INSPIRING PERSONALITY

Is it rare to find individuals with the good qualities mentioned above? Although such educators are exceptional, they do exist. Perhaps more important than looking for inspired individuals is to realize that anyone can become an inspiring personality with effort. Once Sarkar was asked why he did not recruit only the intellectual and well-established personalities for his works. His simple reply was: "What would be the inspiration in that?" Inspiring persons never consist of finished products; rather they make consistent efforts. It is educators' intentions and motives as well as their efforts that allow them to reach these qualities. Sarkar knew that guided by noble principles and through spiritual practices, particularly meditation, a person would move steadily forward.

To become an inspired personality, Neo-humanists view a regular meditation practice as essential. Meditation here refers to a process of contemplating oneself as an expression of loving Infinite Consciousness. This implies the desire to make an inner connection with an unlimited source of greatness. Like a drop of water in a river merging back into the ocean, in meditation one aspires to merge into Infinite Consciousness. In meditation a person systematically reconstructs the energy of each mental layer to merge in the next more subtle layers. The conscious level unites with the subconscious, and then the subconscious joins the unconscious. Ultimately, the meditator intends to merge into the Infinite Consciousness beyond all the layers of the mind.

Many benefits accompany a regular meditative practice such as greater acumen and concentration. When teachers meditate regularly, they become calmer and more attuned to their children's needs. Meditation also gives people heightened awareness of their personal needs for growth and balance. It provides a way to rejuvenate daily.

Having conviction in the Neo-humanistic principles, as well as adopting a meditation practice, ensures growth. Growth consists of a definite part of a teacher's life. Moreover, educators know that others can progress in this way as well. This knowledge gives confidence to educators to encourage others. Some people are diamonds in the mud. They require picking up and cleaning so that one day they will shine brightly. By mentoring individuals who sincerely want to improve their character through the tenets of Neo-humanism and through a meditation practice, one will bear fruit. Any individuals who, after knowing what a life of service entails, apply themselves receive success and self-evolution. Children will see their teachers transform in front of them, which will set off a transformation in their students. Neo-humanism and meditation act as a catalyst to stir up personal and social change and does not let people stagnate as long as they make sincere efforts.

When teachers embody good qualities and live spiritual lives, they have the capacity to inspire and lead others, especially little children. Following the tenets of Neo-humanism and implementing them personally every day in life, enkindles inspiration. Inspiration differs from providing information. Inspiration sets aglow another. The depth inside an inspired teacher touches the core of another, and good things begin to happen. Teaching has many subtleties, and most of them come from a mysterious factor, the inspirational element.

LEADERSHIP CAPACITY

Only people who possess such qualities as integrity, strength of character, righteousness, a sense of social service, unselfishness, and an inspiring personality qualify to be the leaders of children. The real meaning of the word to 'educate' comes from its latent root "educere" to "lead out." Teachers who embody these qualities can "lead out" their children's latent potential to make the children more complete human beings, physically, mentally, and spiritually. They are true leaders, and they inspire, not force. Philosopher Swami Vivekananda urged,

> "One cannot teach a child anymore than one can grow a plant. The plant develops its own nature. The child teaches itself. But a teacher can help it go forward its own way. What one can do is take away the obstacles and fragments, and knowledge comes out naturally. Loosen the soil a little, put a hedge around it and see that it is not killed by anything. Teachers can supply the growing seed, the materials for the making up of its body, bring to it some of the mental materials, and the child will take all that it wants, naturally. A child educates itself. The teacher spoils everything by thinking that he is teaching, for within people stands all knowledge; it requires only awakening, rearranging all the links of thought in the mind, and discovering new links among them. The awakening is the work of the teacher. One has only to do so much for the students that they may learn to apply their own intellect."[9]

Real teaching is setting an example and facilitating a child's efforts. Role modeling is only successful when a teacher's character is noble. Children deserve teachers who embody the noblest qualities of humanity. A teacher not actively pursuing personal improvement and spiritual growth cannot hearten children and motivate them towards Neo-humanism. For it is by their own inspiring example that teachers further students' endeavors. This becomes a starting point and the anchor of a Neo-humanist educator. When the right people do the right work in the right way, the children grow up just right. Individuals with noble qualifications have the right to become teachers; degrees do not automatically make them ones. They must work quickly and effectively, providing knowledge, arranging the environment, and helping children develop their physical, mental, moral, and spiritual aspects. With young children, at the most potential and critical time of their lives, teachers' efforts have lasting effects. Before teachers accept the responsibility of guiding children, they have to look deep inside to determine whether they qualify for this work.

OTHER QUALIFICATIONS

Aside from character and academic criteria, other aspects to a teacher's qualifications exist in Neo-humanism. While setting an ideal example still stands as the single most important role of a teacher, other skills need consideration. Particularly needed are skills such as observation and the ability to create a good learning environment. The teacher needs to develop the skill of being a good observer in order to gain an understanding of each child's progress and growth, including a child's joys and pains. Observation also lets a teacher know which activities and programs work and which do not work. With this understanding they plan, carry out, and assess their teaching. Additionally, teachers have the responsibility of setting up a stimulating environment and using equipment to facilitate children's development. Teachers assist children's development by providing a creative learning environment where children have opportunities to explore. They create a safe environment that is conducive to originality and risk taking.

ADVOCATING

If all the teaching tasks mentioned earlier did not already seem huge, educators' responsibilities go still further. They honor the commitment to the field of education as a whole by helping other educators. Additionally, they acknowledge a larger duty to society. They advocate for Neo-humanism, for young children, and for their families' welfare. With such a tremendous amount of responsibilities, teachers own the title "professional." As a professional, the children, parents, and community expect they can rely on the teacher's astute decisions and best efforts. To handle this complex and evolving role, teachers make a regular push to continuously expand their knowledge, realizing that every personal and professional advance will enhance their children and others directly and indirectly. Being professional means becoming an integral part of a community, not being in isolation. How true and vital the proverb, "It takes a whole village to raise a child." Each educator needs to seek out a support system and a clear way to advance personally and professionally. Neo-humanist teachers, in particular, require keeping company with other similar good-hearted individuals to gain support and strength. With such an important role, Neo-humanist educators have to join with others to improve themselves and to gain strength in order to carry on and do their best.

THE RIGHT TO FORM POLICY

Sarkar went one step further in acknowledging teachers; they "must be given the right to formulate educational policies."[10] As teachers represent those with the most expertise in the field of education, they perform best the job of formulating school policies. Unfortunately, politics and big business often control education policies and funding. Too many times, schools fall prey to special interest groups and factionalism within these powers. Under such circumstances teachers find difficulties in implementing greater ideals. Instead, if freed from pressure from various interest groups, teachers could find new solutions and better methods to improve the education system. They could create an ideal process for children and work without hindrance towards higher ideals. In the mainstream of education today, education fails to adequately support children. While teachers working in public schools generally feel alone and unsupported in their efforts to improve the educational process, in Neo-humanist schools, teachers do not stand-alone but belong to a greater mission. They work along side others to evolve the educational process and share their knowledge with others.

Despite the many educational responsibilities, above all else, educators realize that their work revolves around the axis of their own example. Every aspect of teachers' life impacts the lives of their children because children scrutinize every detail of their teachers' behavior. Consequently, the thoughts, words, and actions of teachers have to be congruent, and they need to keep their character impeccable and exemplary. Teachers constantly convey who they really are and what they believe. Only by leading Neo-humanistic lives can they best accomplish this great task. As the guardians of their young charges, they understand the task of guiding and ennobling their students. To state most simply, Sarkar summarized, "In order to mold a salutary conception of the world in the child, the most important thing that is necessary is stout idealism."[11]

PRECIOUS IS THE CHILD

> *There exists a parallelism between a child and the lotus flower.*
> *Although the lotus stands rooted in muddy waters, its petals remain above smooth and dry. Similarly, if adults know how precious children are and how to best guide them,*
> *They could enjoy the beauty of their flower-like minds.*

There is a great difference in how a teacher guides a child of three years and in how a teacher guides a child of twelve years. In discussing Neo-humanist education effectively, there must be a focus on specific ages. This book centers on Neo-humanist education for the very young children, that is children from birth through eight years old. It covers the early childhood portion of Neo-humanist education.

Unfortunately, early childhood education in general occupies a fairly new position in the educational field, although it has old roots. Even after Freud introduced the concept that vital emotional development occurs at an early age, many at large still persist in looking at children under the age of six as being too young to learn. What people believe about young children makes a difference. Do they see the child as a blank page for a teacher to fill? Do they see the child as a cocoon anticipating birth into a butterfly? Or do they realize that young children have vast, stored knowledge already? Great harm can occur if people see little that is special in early childhood, if they mistake preschool years as being merely an immature stage. The extent educators accurately perceive the depths of their students depends on the educators' own belief system. It is as if each educator wears tinted glasses colored by upbringing, philosophy, and views. Educators interact with young children and value them according to their beliefs. More importantly, belief systems effect teachers' commitments to children.

Neo-humanistic education concludes that children have unlimited potentials and an innate desire to learn. A precept of Neo-humanism is the belief in the child's own motivation to self-actualize. Some educators do not trust and respect children. Trust and respect come from the basic premise that a child has an innate desire to learn and mature. Neo-humanist teachers accept that the child's thirst for knowledge is natural, and they recognize that a wealth of potential lies in every child. Teaching digs for uncovered "gold" and precious "jewels" hidden in children. Children need assistance in comprehending their true and complete selves and in building a proper belief system.

Education theorists recognize the magnitude of the concept that early childhood is the most malleable period of human life. Recent discoveries about the brain indicates that during the period in the womb and throughout the first six years of a child's life ninety percent of an individual's entire personality is formed. Future character and intelligence is mainly derived from the first years of life. In these six initial years, the building of interconnections between the nerve cells in the brain take place. Much of this network of brain patterns come as the result of a child's sensory-motor activity in the physical world. The more extensive and varied the interaction, the greater the capacity for accelerated functions.

Sarkar recognized the subtlety of the early childhood stage. Aside from the latest research, he added other perspicacious elements. Young children, he said, have access to extra-cerebral memory.

> "In the case of a child, since the crude experiences are relatively few, the subtle mind remains tranquil. Thus the waves of the causal mind can easily surface in the child's

subtle mind. As a result, the accumulated experiences of the child's previous life can easily be recollected. This extra-cerebral memory begins to fade after five years. The more one advances in age, the more the new environment leaves it impressions in the child's mind. The more a child sees new things before his eyes, the more restless he becomes to know each and every object of this world. Hence, the child asks a multitude of questions - it seems there is no end to their inquisitiveness. The more they receive the answers to their questions, the more their mind gets acquainted with the mundane world. The experiences of the crude mind then begin and become reflected in the dream-state. As a result, the vibrations of the causal mind cannot come to the surface any more. Hence, the more children advance in age, the more they forget their past lives."[12]

The physiological reasons for this is that the corpus collosum has not fully matured and divided the hemispheres of the brain. This will happen at the age of six. From a linguistic view, as children increasingly adopt more language and other non-verbal symbols of the adult world around them, gradually children learn to interpret and conform within acceptable standards. Neo-humanists explain it psychologically, saying that the more a young child accumulates experiences, the more muddied becomes the surface of the subconscious mind, disabling its perception of the deeper layers. Neo-humanist educators support young children's efforts to gain their present identity, knowledge of the world, and spiritual potentials. While children sort out reality and fantasy, the past and the present, Neo-humanist teachers appreciate the vulnerability and uniqueness of their age.

"AGE APPROPRIATE"

An educator wants to maximize the development of the child in the tender years. Several considerations exist when creating a program for young children. First, the activity of children in early childhood has to be "age and stage appropriate." What is "age appropriate"? Through much research, primarily by cognitive theorists, educators know that children go through universal developmental stages. These stages occur regardless of what culture the child lives in or whether the child rates as a genius, retarded, or of average intelligence. Children may vary in when and how quickly they go through each stage, but they all grow in specific developmental stages. Teachers use "age appropriate" techniques when they understand the universal stages of young children. Educators know what skills unfold at different ages and arrange for suitable activities to advance their children. For instance, Jean as a toddler began to resist adult authority. Jean suddenly understood the consequence of the word "no" and frequently used it. His parents became amazed at how such a previously pliant child now insisted on which food, clothes, or toys he wanted. Their doctor told them this was natural for toddlers and "age appropriate." The doctor advised them to encourage rather than suppress Jean's efforts to become more independent such as to allow Jean to feed and dress himself despite the increase in messiness and time. By encouraging his efforts at independence, Jean would formulate a stronger self-identity.

In many cases, a child may be a certain age but may developmentally act as if in a different stage. Some children leap ahead while other children lag behind in the activities appropriate for their age. Sometimes toddlers incorporate an extraordinary amount of language ability for their age. In this case an activity such as a preschool song becomes more appropriate than a toddler's nursery rhyme. For another toddler the advanced song may be "inappropriate." Children exist as unique individuals, and educators have to be aware of each child's growth rate. If an educator forces a child to speed through or skip a certain stage, the child's learning is impeded. Good educators attempt to make curriculum reach all the ages and stages of the children in their class.

In addition to maturing through stages, Sarkar saw young children's minds as naturally integrated. He saw that every experience effects many areas of the young children's development. For instance, children running together make up an activity that impacts not only physical development but social and emotional development as well. Young children's experiences shape their personality and impact the rest of life. A teacher's care affects children's entire being – physically, mentally, and spiritually in their present and future. Essentially, children's self and worldview comes from this early period.

DEVELOPING THE SELF AND WORLDVIEW

Self-concepts begin evolving in the womb and continue after birth. Self-concepts come as a result of the child's accumulation of experiences with other people and the environment. Most researchers agree that at birth infants do not know what exists as internal or external. Infants discover gradually that their mothers and they have separate bodies. Throughout early childhood, children quickly see more similarities between things than differences. Children eagerly point out more objects of the same color than objects of different colors. If most of the child's interactions contain positive experiences, a positive self-image results. In cases where neglect, rigid discipline, or humiliation occurs, children feel less likeable and unworthy and find fault with themselves and others. Most of these children do not suffer one extreme event of disrespect or one eroding occurrence, but a multitude of many diminishing experiences.

Healthy infants with well met needs readily feel they are a part of a larger whole. They exhibit a natural tendency to show mutual affection. In other words, healthy children show eagerness to expand their 'self' and worldview when they realize their family appreciates their individuality. In a wholesome family, as a baby grows gradually the baby will move to the periphery of the family circle with the other members rather than remain at the center. When children's life is secure, they enjoy the association of others and the family as a whole. This adjustment directly results from the children's pleasure in daily interactions, the children's having their needs well met, and the children's contributions being appreciated. When they grow older, the children perceive themselves as constructive members of society.

On the other hand, if parents do not care well for infants' basic physical and emotional needs, the uncertainty and trauma can cause them to develop less wholesome survival patterns. The instability causes the infants to cling to the center-position in the family. These children do not feel clear about where their emotional boundaries begin and end. Unfortunately, they grow up to be adults who perceive the world overly colored by their own feelings. For instance, they believe when they feel fine that the world appears safe, but when they become depressed, the whole world seems gloomy. The first years of life have an extreme life-forming effect on the self and the worldview.

Despite being faultless, young children often blame themselves for the troubles in the lives of their significant adults. They reduce parental problems into simple terms such as "Mother and Father are fighting because I did not eat my peas." Young children rarely blame others when problems occur. In particular, the more vulnerable and less secure children are the more they blame themselves. Children do not stop there, they extend the stress and insecurity they feel to their life outlook because they believe the world must be the same as their experience. This tendency in young children becomes a growing concern due to the escalation of family stress, for instance the increase in the rate of divorces. Traumatic or diminishing experiences hinders children from developing finer characters and from reaching better intelligence.

Children require clear and consistent messages that give positive feelings and help them gain good self-images. Children learn this through the feeling of acceptance and belonging that comes from others. They want unconditional love and acceptance from their family, and they perceive this approval from others through nonverbal and verbal cues. Although parents remain the key educators of young children, in cases of a dysfunctional family the school becomes increasingly important to the formation of a child's character and intelligence. In schools where children attend classes many hours on a regular basis, teachers' acceptance of each child becomes crucial. Unhappy children and children who have adjustment problems require special inclusion. Adults need to give total and unconditional recognition to every child; any favoritism or disinterest can do harm to the young children in their care. Adults have to make periodic self-assessments on whether they convey acceptance to each child in their care. Take, for instance, the story *Three Letters from Teddy* by an unknown author.

> Teddy was an unattractive child with hair that covered his ears and fell into his eyes. Not only was he behind in academics, he was plain slow and I began to withdraw from him. Ashamed as I admit it, I took a perverse pleasure in using my red pen to mark mistakes on his papers. My cross marks were a little larger and redder than necessary. Reviewing his school records verified how unmotivated he was:
>
> 1st grade: Teddy shows promise with his work and attitude, but he has a poor home environment.
> 2nd grade: Teddy could work better. Teddy's mother is terminally ill. He receives little help at home.
> 3rd grade: Teddy is a pleasant boy, but too serious. He is

a slow learner. His mother passed away end at the end of the year.

4th grade: Teddy is very slow, but well behaved. His father shows no interest.

"Four times he passed, but I will certainly make him repeat fifth grade," I say to myself.

At Christmas time the children brought presents for their teacher. Teddy brought her a gift wrapped in brown paper with red balls and faces colored all over. It read "For Miss Thompson – From Teddy."

All the children were completely silent, they watched while I unwrapped that gift. As I removed the last bit of tape, two items fell to my desk, a ruby rhinestone bracelet with several stones missing and a bottle of cheap perfume. Other children began to laugh at his gift, but I placed the bracelet on my wrist saying, "Teddy, would you help me fasten it?" He smiled shyly as he fixed the clasp, and I held up my wrist for all to admire. There were a few hesitant oohs and aahs, but as I dabbed the cologne, all the girls lined up for a dab behind their ears.

At the end of the day Teddy lingered behind and said, "Miss Thompson, you smell just like Mom. Her bracelet looks real pretty on you, too. I'm glad you like my presents." He left quickly. I locked the door, sat down at my desk, and wept, resolved to make up to Teddy what I had deliberately deprived him of, a teacher who cared.

I stayed every afternoon with Teddy until the last day of school. Slowly, but surely, he caught up with the rest of class and did not have to repeat the fifth grade. In fact, his final averages were among the highest in the class. Although Teddy was moving out of the state when school was out I was not worried, as he had reached a level that would stand him in good stead the following year.

I did not hear from Teddy until seven years later, when the first letter appeared in my mailbox.
Dear Miss Thompson;
I wanted you to be the first to know. I will be graduating second in my class.
Very truly yours, Teddy Stallard
Four years later, another note came.
Dear Miss Thompson:
I wanted you to be the first to know. I was just informed that I'll graduate first in my class. The university has not been easy, but I liked it.
Very truly yours, Teddy Stallard
And now today Teddy's third letter:
Dear Miss Thompson:
I wanted you to be the first to know. As of today, I am Theodore J. Stallard, M.D. How about that? I'm going to be married on July 27th. I want you to come and sit where my mother would sit if she were alive. I'll have no family there as Dad died last year.
Very truly yours, Teddy Stallard
Miss Thompson will proudly go and she was honored that she had done something for Teddy that he could never forget.

WAYS TO STRENGTHEN A CHILD'S SELF IMAGE

Once teachers realize the impact they can have over their children, they ask an important question. What are practical ways to help a child form a positive self-concept? Many opportunities arise to help children know acceptance. For instance, teachers who greet the children warmly when they arrive make children feel welcome. How wonderful when teachers say, "I'm happy to see you." If children are absent, a good teacher tells them they were missed when they return. When children's names are used frequently this sustains children's self-awareness. Teachers should avoid referring to children by groups. Instead of saying, "You girls in the corner" say, "Mary, Sally, and Marie." When teachers offer positive reinforcement, they assist children in establishing good self-identities.

In conveying personal recognition, non-verbal cues carry more weight than words. The tone of voice and body language conveys more meaning than what is said. Does the adult look into the child's face with a smile, with a bored expression, or with exasperation? An adult's face gives myriad cues to children as to whether they like or dislike the children. Touch and nearness provide other important signs to preschoolers. Sensitive teachers learn much about the state of their children's state of being through physical expression. A non-verbal signal such as eye contact makes up one of the most poignant messages. By making good eye contact, the children let the teacher know that they welcome their teacher into their world. Research shows that the more people like someone, the more they look at them. By not looking at an adult, the children tell with their eyes that they do not give them admittance to their world. If the teacher takes the time to individually interact with each child, it dispels many of the child's tensions and fears.

Neo-humanist teachers want to fully support children's acceptance and appreciation of themselves. Teachers look for different cues that children offer about themselves. By observing the children in various ways such as looking at their artwork and watching what type of roles they take during dramatic play, teachers learn much about the child's self-image. Teachers talk and listen to children about their home life and make notes of their observations and discussions. This should provide clues as to the child's level of self-acceptance.

Many activities facilitate children's efforts to accept themselves. Particularly, imaginative activities such as visualization and silence games facilitate children's discovery of their inner selves. Other activities such as looking at mirrors, photos, and taping children's voices help establish the children's self-identity. Any activity that allows children to feel interested and successful builds the child's confidence. Children want to feel successful in class activities. When children perceive an activity as being too hard, they are soon disheartened. On the other hand, when children find activities too easy, they quickly lose interest. It is their feeling of success that motivates them to continue with the activity and to try a new one.

Teachers have to know their children well and their children's different strengths and weaknesses to plan activities that allow each child to mature successfully. Children vary in their physical, mental, social, emotional, and spiritual abilities. Teachers need vigilance to meet each child's personal needs. This task can become overwhelming; however, an educator has the golden opportunity to facilitate and assist children to become greater. Similar to an explorer, every educator needs to discover their children's potentials and to uncover the precious jewels that are in each.

THE AWAKENING OF SPIRIT

A parent hands a young child beautiful flowers to decorate the family altar.
Tiny hands quiver with delight and wonder, play-acting with solemn seriousness.

Neo-humanist education values the spiritual qualities of the child. Education does not consist of a dry process of information giving and memorization, rather it is seen as a flowering of the mind and heart. Sarkar told:

> "The aim of education is: "Sa vidya' ya' vimuktaye"- Education is that which liberates. The real meaning of education is trilateral development – simultaneous development in the physical, mental, and spiritual realms of human existence. This development should enhance the integration of the human personality. By this, dormant human potentialities will be awakened and put to proper use."[13]

Spirituality is a fundamental concept of Neo-humanist education. Neo-humanist teachers live inspiring lives through meditation and through contemplation of salient ideals and by relating these to their work in education. Commonly, spirituality refers to making a connection or relation to Infinite Consciousness, which is both within and beyond the physical, psychic, and psycho-spiritual realms. Although the Infinite Consciousness essentially is everywhere, how to realize this? Sarkar explained,

"Who is your nearest person? You try to know so many things, but you should know first of all your nearest object. What is your nearest object? Your hands? Your fingers? No, no, no. Your arms? No, no, no. Your chest? No, no, no. What is the nearest point? Your "I" is your nearest entity. And the distance cannot be measured. First of all you should know all the characteristics of your own "I."[14]

"For each and every human being there are two "I's." The name of a person, say, is Solomon. Then the name of his little "I" is Solomon and the name of his big "I" is that Supreme Entity. The name of the little "I" is Mr. Joseph, but the name of his big "I" is the Supreme Consciousness. The big "I" for all created beings is the same, but the little "I" varies – so many bodies having so many names. The big "I" is one and indivisible: for the entire universe there is one big "I."[15]

Any spiritual practice aims to convert the little "I" into the big "I." During meditation people focus on their "I feeling", and then super-impose the idea that they are part of the loving Infinite Consciousness over their small "I feeling." Inevitably, with sincere effort the little "I" becomes greater and more spiritual. While young children do not have the maturity to practice real meditation, they can learn to begin to keep a quiet time in which they introvert their thoughts and become more self-aware. Teaching spirituality in schools begins with encouraging children to evolve the power of internal reflection and self-control during a regular quiet time. Teachers may introduce simple visualization and centering games that may eventually interest them in meditation. Assuredly, whether a young child really thinks about love or similar ideas that lead to true meditation cannot be certain. By keeping a regular quiet time, though, they develop an internal awareness that assists spiritual development. Teachers set aside a special time to support internal reflection. Different schools may call the meditative period by various terms such as "silence game", "inner time", "centering" or the "time to find a secret place inside where you feel safe and peaceful". What the teacher names it has less significance than the imbibing of it with a spirit of reverence. Carefully the teacher introduces, conducts, and concludes the reflective period to make it special for the children.

Beginning the meditative time can be done in various ways to channel the children's energy and to generate a feeling of group solidarity. Methods include singing songs, telling stories, warm-up exercises, discussion, and creative movement. Just before the silence game, teachers choose an activity that assures calmness. Then they ask children to become very peaceful by putting their hands in their laps, sitting still and tall, and closing their eyes. Together the teacher and children sing or chant loudly, gradually softening their voices until they whisper. Teachers tell the children to whisper so quietly that no one else can hear it. Young children find the transition between whispering to listening to their internal voice helpful.

For young children, talking about a personal thought that culminates in silence can enhance their reflective experience. For instance, the educator employs simple visualizations that end in a silent period: "Visualize your mother; feel the love you feel for your mother and that your mother feels for you; keep your eyes closed and allow that love to surround you and fill you. Your mother is whispering you a song of love." Other imaginative thoughts that help children are colorful metaphors that arouse spiritual feelings. For instance, a teacher named June told her preschoolers to imagine they were mountains. In a quiet voice she said, "Be like a giant, monolithic rock. Close your eyes; sit straight and tall like a mountain with your head touching the clouds. Feel the wind gently blow around you. The wind blows around and around you. Let the wind whisper inside your heart its song of love."

Developing metaphoric visualizations around learning themes gives teachers wonderful tools to add spiritual and creative depth to the curriculum. For instance when children study about space and the night sky the teacher can ask them to close their eyes and make their minds as vast as space. The teacher says, "See myriad stars shining and watching you. "Remember you are never alone or helpless. The force that guides the stars guides you too."[16]

When June's preschool children studied about fire they cooked, painted, and read about it. She created an imaginative visualization around an inspirational passage, "The flame of a lamp lights up countless lamps."[17] During quiet time June lit a candle for the children and asked them to describe it. After the children had gazed for awhile, June asked them to close their eyes. "With your eyes closed can you still see the candle in your mind, burning with a bright and colorful flame? Fire when cared for makes us warm and bright as a friend. One little light can light many candles."

There are no limits to the exciting and imaginative ideas that children can visualize. When children study about water, they can imagine being a river, flowing over rocks and stones towards the ocean. The teacher tells the children, "Hear the ocean as you flow happily to meet it. Greatness calls you in the thunder of the waves." During the theme on dinosaurs children can imagine themselves as sleeping old, huge dinosaurs. Teachers say, "You are such an old and ancient dinosaur. While you are sleeping as a big dinosaur you begin to dream. You dream about how old you are. You are the oldest creature. Then you dream that before you there existed an ancient time where things were still and peaceful, the most ancient, hoary time." With practice, teachers can create interesting metaphors and visualizations to stimulate the deeper and spiritual natures of the children.

The post-meditative moment is as important as the contemplative time. Teachers utilize the post-meditative atmosphere to channel the children's subtle energy in different ways. It is effective to follow reflection with subtle experiences such as watering and kissing a plant, sharing news, or practicing children's yoga. Other charming activities include giving, from one to another, an imaginary object such as light or a fairy, passing small objects such as a feather or a chestnut, or handing out raisins.

Spiritual stories after meditative times highlight and exemplify spiritual qualities in a manner that is enjoyable and easy for children to grasp. To illustrate, read the following story of "Madalasa," an ancient biography that has inspired and consoled children for centuries.

Hundreds of years ago, there lived a famous woman named Madalasa. When she was young, she did not want to marry but due to her beauty and wisdom a king pursued her. Reluctantly she consented to marry the king but only if he promised to allow her to rear their children by herself. Any interference would end their marriage. Enchanted with Madalasa, the king agreed to allow her to solely educate their children. Over time, the king and Madalasa had three sons. Every day Madalasa sang to her children a Sanskrit lullaby to awaken in them the awareness of their divine nature:

SHUDDHOSI BUDDHOSI NIRAINJANOSI
SAM'SARA MAY'YA' PARIVARJITOSI
SAM'SARA SVAPANAM' TYAJA MOHA NIDRAM
MADALASA ULASAM' BHAJA MOHA NITYAM.

You are pure, intuitional, and unblemished.
Shun the illusions of this world.
Wake up from the dream of this material world.
Madalasa's children, remember upon this day in and day out.

Under her careful guidance, the first two sons developed into good and pious men, but neither wanted to be king. The king became sad and angry when his two eldest sons refused to become kings. He decided he had to raise the last son to become a king, and he took him away from Madalasa. The king named the boy "Alarka," which means mad dog, to discourage godliness. As per their agreement Madalasa left her husband, but before departing she gave Alarka a ring with a hidden message. Carefully she instructed that only at his darkest hour should he read it.

Alarka grew up under his father's tutelage and became a ruthless king. The people hated him and they joined a neighboring king to dethrone him. Defeated and homeless, Alarka walked in despair alone in the forest. One day Alarka looked at the ring his Mother left him and decided to read her message. Inside he found: "Best is no desire, but if this is too difficult desire only God. Best is no company, but if this is too hard keep only holy company." With those words and her memory, he began his spiritual path; one day becoming a sage.

Spiritual stories enliven higher concepts and help the children catch them quickly. Children love the medium of inspirational stories, and beg for more stories from their teacher. The use of stories and other methods to enhance children's spiritual awareness effectively enriches their lives. When children sense an open and spiritual atmosphere, they may spontaneously ask teachers questions such as "Where is heaven?" "What happens if I sleep and do not wake up?" which springboards higher learning. True education occurs when teachers value and count spirituality as an integral part of education. Young children are open toward these concepts. If teachers show reasonable regard and care toward spiritual ideas, children easily grasp them and desire for its mysteries. They will want to find that the one, loving Infinite Consciousness as their dearest companion. As an ancient saying says,

> "O Child! Do not disregard this enlivening love of your Supreme friend. Do not allow any of His gifts to go useless. Pay heed to his words with a steady mind. O child! Do not forget how much He has done for you, how much He is doing, and how ready He is to do anything for you."[18]

UNIVERSAL LOVE

"All the year round she kept racks full of plants in pots standing on green painted wooden steps. There were rare geraniums, dwarf rosebushes, spiraeas with misty white and pink plume."

Colette [19]

Closely related to spirituality is the belief in Universalism. Perceiving that behind the play of innumerable forms exists Infinite Consciousness makes life sweeter. With a little imagination people see a tree as a living poem, instead of a tool to exploit. Universalism means extending the mental and emotional boundaries of concern, respect, and affection people reserve for humanity towards minerals, plants, and animals. It makes up the broadest possible outlook. Each individual should be nurtured and respected in every situation. For instance, author Jack Canfield described an incident involving his neighbors in *Chicken Soup for the Soul*.

> One day his neighbor was teaching his seven-year-old son how to push a lawn mower. For a moment, while his son was cutting the grass, the father turned his attention elsewhere and the son mowed through a flowerbed. Angrily the father began to scold his son, but his wife came over and put her hand on her husband's shoulder saying, "Please remember ... we're raising children, not flowers." Immediately, the father softened. With a few choice words, she reminded her husband to cherish their child.[20]

Neo-humanists understand children are precious and additionally add, "everything is dear." In the above story the father could say, "Son, I know that learning to mow is exciting, but it includes a responsibility. Those flowers you cut want to live and grow as much as you and I." Universalism expands human love into universal love that includes all forms and bestows the highest regard towards everything. In Neo-humanism, equally important is the significance of each individual and their interconnectedness.

In the past, educational theories confined themselves to human concerns only. Various educational theorists discussed human love and mutual respect. They accepted that children regardless of their culture, race, or religion deserve good care and education. Sarkar, though, explains in Neo-humanism that education exists for all beings, not only human beings. This creates a different worldview that impacts various aspects of education. When people accept the significance and inter-relatedness of life, they see themselves as caretakers, seeing to the wellbeing of others. Intellectual advancement alters when it extends to valuing others, not only human beings, but also other living beings such as animals and plants. Neo-humanist education accepts Universalism and seeks ways to transfer this concept and feeling to the children. For instance, in the playground a group of children broke off a tree branch. Susan, their teacher, asked the children how they would feel to be a tree and have their branches broken. Would it feel pleasant or hurt? The children said it would hurt. She asked the children to go and hug the tree, which they gladly did. Susan noticed their energy changed from rough and callous to considerate and joyful after this.

The attitude children form towards people, animals, and things influences their future lives. These attitudes determine how children interrelate with society. The attitudes influence the choices the children make. For example, Dr. Stephen Keller of Yale University found that children who abuse animals have a much higher likelihood of becoming violent criminals. Evidence suggests that people who learned to care for plants and animals as children had more responsibility and empathy as they matured.[21]

Young children require assurance and guidance towards caring for and loving the world around them. An understanding of the spirit of Universalism engenders children with a foundation to become responsible, caring, and beneficial members of society. Unfortunately, many education theories do not value Universalism and exhort different messages. Goading children to compete and seek promotion over others, other theories look primarily at academic advancement and social prestige. Author Richard J. Barnet describes the process of changing people's outlook to one of caring for others. He states:

> "Stewardship requires a capacity to feel the pain and to share the joy of people who live at a great distance. People do not practice conservation unless they see a compelling purpose and can envision the flesh-and-blood beneficiaries of their sacrifice."[22]

> "Our educational establishment inoculates us against empathy. The survival values our society prizes are individualist. We are trained to be cerebral, thick-skinned, and obsessed with ourselves. These are not the survival values of a world of scarcity."[23]

With Neo-humanism, children learn to empathize, to put themselves in the place of another, whether the other is human or not. By encouraging children not only to empathize with other people but with the environment as well, they mature into responsible adults. Helping children to become universal enables them to more fully care for others and become amenable towards them.

LEARNING STRATEGIES

Children learn from watching and imitating adults. Children notice the smallest and most unconscious actions. Teachers and parents continuously must ask themselves, "What am I showing this child? Is the child learning Neo-humanism? Have I instilled this child a respect for the environment?" How do I care for animals or insects? If a child kills a spider or gecko, how do I react? Do I recycle and compost? Adult modeling implants on the impressionable minds of young children, shaping their outlook.

Besides modeling, teachers seek out learning opportunities to encourage greater empathy in children. If a child kills a spider, they talk about how the spider did not want to die and how it helps the garden. When children catch little creatures, teachers emphasize that the children have to take care while handling the living things and then return these creatures to their environment after observation.

Opportunities unfold when teachers go into nature with the children. For instance the class can visit trees and discuss their parts and how they grow, observing details such as whether the trees have new leaves and what creatures live in them. The teachers can set up gardening activities such as sprouting seeds. Some schools have yards and areas for large pots to make up vegetable gardens. By regular gardening at school children increase their awareness of nature and nature's reciprocal relationship. Cultivation of plants shows children that patience brings a joyful reward. Additionally, the school can make a compost heap in conjunction with the growing of plants. After a while the compost becomes food for the children's plants. In some cases an outside garden is not possible, for instance a teacher named Melody had a class in an inner city area with many disruptive children. These children needed more immediate returns from gardening then waiting for seeds to grow. Melody requested each child to bring a potted plant to school that they would care for each day. Some plants that the children brought did not have adequate pots and soil. She arranged for those children to replant them and gave them fertilizer. Each had to give their plant a pet name. The children came up with funny names such as Mr. Green, Floppy, and Monster or gave them human names.

As a writing activity the children made fancy name tags for their plants. Daily the children watered them with water spray bottles. Not only did the children learn to appreciate plants, the greenery enlivened the classroom's atmosphere.

Stories make an excellent medium to convey complex ecological ideas. Good stories enable children to learn about how to care for the environment. Educators can easily make up their own stories or adapt stories to fit an ecological theme. For example, follows the story, *A Picnic at Ypao Beach* written by Preschool teacher, Ketana Bardwell.

> One Sunday afternoon, Karen and Mark went with their family to Ypao Beach for a picnic. As soon as they arrived they ran to the water. "Let's go swimming!" the two children yelled.
>
> When they were swimming the children saw some fish. Karen said, "Those fish look sick, I think they are sad."
>
> Suddenly, to their surprise, one of the fish spoke, "Once we were happy swimming around the coral. The water was clear. Then people threw trash in the water. First they threw paper and then plastic things. It covered the coral and some fish ate and choked on the plastic. Can you help us?"
>
> Karen and Mark felt sorry for the fish. They wondered what could they do to help the fish. Mark said, "We could pick up the trash."
>
> The children began picking up litter. Soon it grew late and dark, but there was still more litter to pick up. Karen and Mark told their mother and father about the fish dying from all the trash. "Please, can you make sure we take all our trash away?" they asked.
>
> Their mother and father helped them pick up the trash. Other people saw them and began to help pick up the garbage. With more people helping, it was easy to pick up the trash.

Regularly, Mark and Karen went to the beach and checked on the fish, picking up trash. People stopped throwing trash in the water and on the beach because the children would tell them about the fish. Soon the fish were feeling better. "Thank-you," said the fish, "you have saved our life."

In general as society races towards the 21st century, people cannot ignore the fragile balance between life. Today's children play an important role in caring for the earth and restoring this balance. For this reason, schools that adopt environmental education as part of the curriculum impart the skills and values necessary for responsible stewardship of the planetary resources. By enabling children to form an intimate, living relationship with the web of life, they learn how to create and sustain a healthier, ecological society. To emphasize the urgency for ecological concern, Sarkar composed many Bengali songs Below is the translation of one of them:

> "Oh human being! Losing your awareness,
> Where are you heading?
> Poisoning the air and the sky,
> Turning the earth into a hell.
> You used to say that you were superior.
> That the animals, birds, and trees were inferior to you
> Don't you see the shadow of time?
> Approaching rapidly
> To stop your speed."[24]

MULTI-CULTURAL APPRECIATION

Neo-humanist education recognizes only Universalism that embraces others, and rejects sentiments such as communalism, racism, and nationalism that impose limitations on the human mind. While recognizing the importance of all life, Neo-humanism confirms the magnificence of diversity. All the various races and cultures of the world, Neo-humanism states, make up a charming and heterogeneous garden.

Education counters dogmatic sentiments and spreads Universalism by creating empathetic connections in children's minds. Basically, children want to understand who they are and who they are not, a complex process throughout life. This starts in infancy when children see a wide range of physical characteristics, from skin and hair colors to shapes of noses and eyes. Later, in middle childhood, children come to understand cultural and political dimensions of race and ethnicity and how these are significant in their lives. While assimilating these similarities and differences, children should believe that all are equal and integral parts of society's garden.

Educators of very young children play an essential role in promoting equality. Numerous studies, from a cognitive development perspective, have shown that infants and preschoolers notice racial cues. In a United States' study, when three to four year olds were shown photos of three people and asked to match the two that were similar, children most often used skin color as the determinant. [25]

When young children develop racial awareness, they acquire language to describe and categorize what they notice based on what they hear from peers and adults. Around age five, children typically can use race or color terms such as black or white and ethnic descriptions such as Chinese and Spanish. Interestingly, research shows young children describe physical differences associated with race before they understand that these categorize people into a specific group.[26]

Educators have to assist children to value differences and to understand these differences as external appearance, whereas our needs are the same. Moreover, children must learn that they are equal to others and appreciate that others can feel the same way as they do, regardless of external dissimilarities. Children understand this by the openness and acceptance they perceive in their school relations, beginning with a sense of belonging and valuing of each other. Good teachers look for "teachable moments" when children spontaneously show curiosity about their own or others' race; for instance, they listen when a young child expresses confusion about a racial term. "Why are people called "Blacks" when they have brown skin?" "Why are people labeled "White" when they are tan and beige?" This may provide an opportunity to share a discussion of people's similarities and differences with the children comparing their skin shades and textures.

Neo-humanist educators want children to believe that they are part of a universal family. The feeling of kinship in a classroom evolves in several ways. Particularly, kinship grows from warm relationships and a sense of belonging. To fully be aware of individual student's needs teachers have to study their children's backgrounds. They can create themes, activities, and teachable moments if they know their students' backgrounds well. One encouraging activity that teachers can easily set up is to lay a large blanket down and pretend with the children that they are going on a magic carpet ride. After reading stories and showing pictures of other places such as Delhi and Manila, the class imagines flying to them on the magic carpet. Then they "travel" to other places that the children request or areas that are tied to the children's history. Afterward, they can draw pictures or build out of blocks a building that they may have imagined on the flying carpet ride. Teachers can become better acquainted with their students' heritage, by offering the students' families a history questionnaire with points such as:

> What is the significance of my naming my child this name?
> Where were my child's maternal grandparents born and raised?
> Where were my child's paternal grandparents born and raised?
> Where were my child's parents born and raised?

What is the family's cultural/ethnic heritage?
What language(s) are spoken at home?
Please describe special customs or traditions of the family?

Depending on the location, each school has its own expressions of culture. On the Micronesian Island of Guam, Ananda Marga Preschool enrolls children with an array of cultural backgrounds such as Chamorro, Filipino, Caucasian, Afro-American, Japanese, and Korean. In other areas schools have less diverse backgrounds, thus the teachers have to work harder to promote a broader awareness in the students. In these areas, teachers support diversity by creating a culturally rich environment by using pictures, cultural objects, and books. A good school setting stimulates the development of Universalism and broadmindedness.

When children of different backgrounds feel comfortable and supported in their cultural growth, the class turns into a haven. Additionally, educators promote the awareness of others in a positive way. When children perceive they are accepted, they delight in learning about the many similarities and differences they have with children from other backgrounds. In setting up a rich and diverse atmosphere, educators have to root out any portrayal of a bias. For instance, the dolls in the classroom need to have different skin colors. They use stories and pictures that portray men and women of various backgrounds doing jobs such as blue collar, pink collar, white collar, and artistic work. Additionally, differently-abled people such as people in wheel chairs or deaf are shown in work and play. More than tourist-like approaches where the children visit another culture only occasionally, educators make a regular effort to integrate awareness and acceptance of diversity in an anti-bias manner.

NEVER CAN GET ENOUGH OF MORALITY

> *"I have a flower for you that I have grown while you were learning how to open the gate."*
> *The fairy added, "This flower will remind you how to live and be happy.*
> *It has ten petals, one for each lesson you learned today."*

The development of good values and ethics makes up a major part of Neo-humanist education, especially education of the very young. Ethical teachings support spirituality and Universalism by providing the "do's and don'ts" of life for daily interactions. Unlike a social code, ethics are innate in every person. More than guidelines, they comprise the intrinsic principles that sit in the human heart. By complying with morality, humanity advances and lives in harmony. Neo-humanism subscribes to the following ten principles of morality.

Ethical concepts	Related values
Non-harming	compassion, friendliness
Benevolent truthfulness	sense of justice, straightforwardness
Non-stealing	trustworthiness, empathy
Universal love	sweetness, caring, openness
Simple living	moderation, balance
Cleanliness of body and mind	genuine, introspective

Contentment	positive outlook, acceptance
Social service	generous, humility
Inspirational study	thoughtful, studiousness
Self-knowledge and spiritual pursuit	sincerity, discipline

When people live ethically, they form strong characters. Yet to develop strong character, takes determination and effort because moral adherence is repeatedly tested. At any moment, a weakness in a person's character can pull the individual in wrong directions. Throughout life, from infancy to old age, morality entails constant effort, yet its inculcation provides great satisfaction.

MORALITY IN EDUCATION

Morality comprises the "do's and "don'ts" or the "abstinence's and observances" of people's behavior and thoughts. According to Sarkar, by the age of five children have formed their moral outlook. He considered it the most essential aspect of early childhood development.

> "In our education system, emphasis should be given to moral education and the inculcation of idealism — not only philosophy and traditions. At all levels the practice of morality should be the most important subject in the syllabus." [27]

Through the medium of stories and dramas, children learn important ethical concepts. Integrity and good qualities are beautifully illustrated in stories. Such stories capture the child's attention and imagination, and brighten their efforts. In the literary world there exist thousands of children's stories, folk tales, and biographical stories that call for children to appreciate values and morality. To illustrate, below is a wonderful story called the Fairy's Flower by an unknown author that incorporates essential moral concepts.

One day Kate went walking into a forest where a beautiful fairy lived. She wanted to meet the fairy as she heard the fairy grew magical flowers, which sometimes she gave as gifts. As Kate walked she heard an owl above her head, "Hoo, you will not find the fairy."

When Kate heard what the owl said, she became angry. Kate picked up a stone and threw it at the owl. The stone hit its wing. "Ouch," squawked the owl and flew away.

Kate kept walking through the forest until she reached a big gate with a silver bell. Ringing the bell, a monkey appeared and said, "Who are you and what do you want?"

"I am Kate and I want to meet the fairy," said Kate.

The monkey told "She never sees anyone who hurts others" and he disappeared.

Kate remembered she hit the owl with a stone. She left the gate and searched for the owl. "Owl, please come out. I am sorry for hurting you." The owl, out of fear, did not appear.

"I have candy in my pocket. If you come out, I will give it to you," she promised. Kate lied, as she had no candy in her pocket.

The owl came out and flew near Kate. "Where is the candy?" asked the owl.

"You can have it later, let's first visit the fairy," Kate said.

So they set off to the fairy's gate. When they reached the gate Kate rang the bell and the monkey appeared. Kate said, "I have brought the owl as a friend. Now can I meet the fairy?"

The monkey told the owl to come inside and said to Kate, "the fairy never sees anyone who tells lies."

Kate set out to find candy to give to the owl as she had promised. After walking for sometime she saw a small house in the woods. She ran as fast as she could and knocked on the door. No one answered. Kate pushed open the door and went inside. She saw pots full of candy sitting on a table. Grabbing a handful of candy, she rushed back to the fairy's gate.

On top of the gate sat the monkey. It looked at Kate and said, "the fairy does not see anyone who takes something without the owner's permission."

So Kate went back to the house where she stole the candy. When she knocked on the door an old woman appeared. "Come in," she said.

"I went into your house when you were not home and took candy without permission. Here is your candy. I'm sorry," said Kate.

Then the old woman smiled saying "Because you have returned my candy I forgive you. Take this pocketful of sugared nuts as a gift from me."

Kate thanked the woman and walked back to the fairy's gate. On her way she saw a little squirrel. It jumped in front of her and said, "Please, I am so hungry. Can you share some food?"

"I have some sweet nuts but I cannot give you any. The owl and I will eat it," answered Kate who kept walking.

When Kate rang the bell the monkey opened the gate. Kate said, "I gave back the candy, and have brought some sugared nuts for the owl. Now can I meet the fairy?"

The monkey took some candied nuts to give to the owl. Then he told, "The fairy does not see anyone who does not care about all creatures and share when they have plenty.

Kate ran back to the squirrel and gave it some candied nuts. She began to appreciate every creature as the fairy's friend.

Quickly Kate walked back to the fairy's gate. She did not see a puddle of mud. Whoops, she fell into it! Kate picked herself up and walked to the fairy's gate.

When the monkey saw her he said, "You look too dirty. Go down the road to the lake and wash before knocking again."

Kate hurried down the road to the lake where she washed off the dirt. On her way back to the fairy's gate she heard a mother deer calling for her baby. The baby had wandered off and was lost. Kate helped the mother deer look for the baby. They found the baby sleeping under a tree. The mother deer was very grateful. Kate, though, was lost in the forest. Kate began to get scared and then stopped. Instead she began to think how beautiful was the forest and about the fairy. With these happy thoughts she found her way again and reached the fairy's gate.

This time the monkey wore a big smile and said, "The fairy was glad that you helped Mother deer and for your happy thoughts. Now she wants you to read this book. Come back later."

Kate sat under a tree and began to read. The book was about the deepest love, written by a wise person. The book urged her to find this love inside her heart.

"I want to find the deepest love," said Kate. She sat very still with her eyes closed. She thought of the fairy's flower. Suddenly she saw a flower in her heart. She sat even stiller, and the flower grew brighter and loving feelings warmed her heart. Joyful tears came down her cheeks.

After some time she stood up and walked to the fairy's gate, which now stood wide open. Kate heard a sweet voice call out, "Welcome, my child!"

She saw a beautiful fairy dressed in a white gown standing by rows of radiant flowers. The fairy called, "Come near, my dear. I grew a flower for you while you learnt how to open the gate. This flower has ten petals, one for each lesson you learned today. What are they?"

Kate answered, "I will not do harm to anyone. I do not lie or steal. I see all creatures as your friends and share with them when I am able." She continued, "I want to be clean and remember happy thoughts. I will help others and read wise books. And most of all, inside my heart is the deepest love growing like a flower. By tending it, the more brightly and lovingly it shines."

The fairy nodded and handed Kate a beautiful flower. Kate held the flower and raised it to smell its sweet fragrance. Suddenly everything disappeared and she found herself on the path to her home, holding a beautiful flower.[28]

This story tells of important principles of morality in a simple manner, understandable to young children. Each petal represents one of the ten universal concepts that have relevance to both adults and children. Stories capture children's interest and make connections to prompt their memories. When teaching children about morality, teachers do not demand children to master these concepts, anymore than they can personally expect to master them in their own life. Instead educators inspire and hope to make a significant difference in the children's moral development through their personal example, stories, and encouragement.

THE TWINGE OF CONSCIENCE

An early starting point in moral guidance consists of urging children to listen to the "uh-oh" and "ah" feelings, the voices of conscience inside them. By listening to their small inner voice they will know when they have or have not made good choices. There are two ways the "twinge of conscience" empowers them. First, it gives them insight to when they have good experiences. In this aspect, the inner small voice says, "ah." Teachers point out to children that when they aid another child or creature, they sense pleasantness in their tummies or hearts. Inside they may hear a small voice say, "ah." Assisting and being kind to another, makes their "ah" impressions resonate with good and happy feelings. When they sense unfairness and unkindness, children should attune to their "uh-oh" feeling. The "uh-oh" feeling aids them in the practice of fairness in play. It gives awareness when they over-step rules or hurt someone. Tuning into this feeling allows them to know it is time to calm down, change to another play, or make amends. Hence, a major goal for young children is the fostering of awareness of conscience and the "ah" and "uh-oh" feelings, as a means to balance their individual needs and wishes with other children's.

To assist children to learn the "ah" and "uh-oh" feelings, a teacher may use group discussion and individual interactions. Teachers introduce the concept during a group discussion. They ask the group if they have a small voice or little feeling inside their tummies and hearts that let them know if something is wrong or right. Children, with some urging, talk about this quite openly. Later, teachers talk with individual students when an interaction such as hitting arises. Teachers ask if the children forgot to stop and hear their "uh-oh" feelings. After calming down, do they feel it now? Young children find this easier to do than adults.

Generally, most of moral education comes through life's lessons, particularly in the trials and errors of daily living. Social interactions especially provide learning opportunities whereby children can strengthen their morality. Good character growth results from open atmospheres that allow experimentation and from teachers guiding children in a friendly manner.

OBSERVING ETHICAL BEHAVIOR

While teaching children about morality, teachers closely watch children to assess their progress. Through observing, teachers note what children do and where they are in their individual development. Observations need to be recorded through anecdotal notes and simple checklists. By monitoring and recording children's progress, the teacher discovers patterns of behavior in their children. In this way the educator can better decide what areas of ethical development need to be focused upon in the case of each student. An example of a simple moral checklist for young children follows:

NON-HARMING
- shows remorse after harming another
- tries to stop others from harming others, including plants or animals

BENEVOLENT TRUTHFULNESS
- looks adult in face while talking
- gives answer without fear (when asked calmly)

NON-STEALING
- returns school toys when finished
- does not pocket or hide another's toy

UNIVERSAL LOVE
- shows care for plants and animals
- shows pleasure for other's happiness and concern for other's distress

SIMPLE LIVING
- shares with others
- easily contented with only a few toys

CLEANLINESS
- Is enthusiastic to wash hands
- when angry, recovers in reasonable time and manner

CONTENTMENT
- recovers from distress in reasonable time
- smiles often

SERVICE-ORIENTED
- shares something they own with another
- helps another do a task

INSPIRATIONAL STUDY
- likes to listen to inspiring stories
- asks many questions

SPIRITUAL PURSUIT
- participates in silence game
- asks spiritual questions

VALUES

Acquainting children with many values constitutes another important step in teaching ethics. Every moral principle when implemented offers positive character values to the child. As children integrate ethical principles into their life, they move away from a "do's and don'ts" perspective. Increasingly, they express various character traits and qualities attributed to the ethical concepts. For example, when children practice non-harming they evolve various traits such as compassion, gentleness, friendliness, and kindness. These qualities become important, and form an integral part of the children's personalities. Another example is found in children who learn to speak on the behalf of other's welfare. They often develop into fine leaders and have qualities such as fairness, decisiveness, and courage. Every ethical concept has many associating values. As P. R. Sarkar says, "Remember when this moralism, on which human existence is based, leads a person to the fullest expression of their finer human qualities, then alone is its practical value properly realized."[29]

Teachers assist young children to learn virtues when they compliment children doing good deeds. If children exhibit patience, the teacher says to them, "You were very patient." When a child assists a fallen friend, the instructor thanks the child for being caring and helpful. When teachers reinforce their qualities at the time of occurrence, children learn these virtues. If a teacher wants to correct children, for instance, children pushing to the head of a line, the teacher says, "I appreciate your wanting to be leaders, but I need you to be patient. Please cooperate by waiting your turn." Here the teacher recognized some virtue in what the children exhibited, but aimed the children toward the required virtue. "I appreciate your enthusiasm, I need you to be considerate right now. Please be helpful and show the younger children how to wait in line." Using the language of virtues in guiding everyday activities assists children in acquiring them.

MODELING

Regardless of how many ideas there exist on guiding children in their moral growth, the key means are an adult's loving behavior and good role modeling. Children constantly watch adults for cues as to what to do and how to act. Many times a child's home may be chaotic and dysfunctional, and the school becomes the arena where the child receives good examples and finds acceptance. Only if teachers live ethically can they be authentic models for the children. If the teacher's behavior reflects good values, the children strive harder towards morality. To really model good values, teachers have to truly be inspired by superior moral concepts in their own lives. Focusing on good values and morals must be an active process in their personal interactions. Referring to the fairy's flower, each one must genuinely own this flower before they can inspire others. The more radiant their flower, the more charming and attractive their example.

Morality is the most important aspect of the curriculum, and children learn morality by integrating it in many ways. Besides modeling ethical behavior, teachers offer exemplary stories and acknowledge when their students demonstrate values and moral conduct. Morality cannot be an isolated lesson; rather, teachers incorporate it into every aspect of the educational process. Teachers assist children in every way to acquire ethics during the early years of life.

TEARS AND SMILES OF EMOTIONAL GROWTH

Little, Princess, there are many flowers
Why this rose you remember more?
God called me to this rose
When the tide shifts, to the next bloom I will go.
What of that red rose?
Will it wither and its perfume fade?
Nay, the rose will be in Thy garland
Safely, where it belongs.

Closely inter-related to children's moral progress is their emotional health. Strict adherence to moral principles results in greater expression of joy, fortitude, contentment, and many other values and qualities. Only through moral behavior can positive expressions grow and deepen. Yet the adherence to morality does not mean that unpleasant feelings disappear. For similarly to the mud that holds a plant, unpleasant occurrences remain as part of life. People who follow morality occasionally experience unpleasant emotions and expressions such as sadness, guilt, and fear. They accept life's expressions in their entirety and then have impetus to resolve or to improve situations. Everyone forges character on the strength of moral fortitude. Using another analogy, moral effort acts as the striking matches or flint, the resultant good qualities and finer feelings shine as brilliant blazes of light, and the general emotions or human expressions represents the rough, hard stone — the base from which people learn. Although emotions relate to ethics, they come from the unaccomplished human side where the battle for self-control keeps being fought.

HUMAN EXPRESSION

Although most people use the word "emotion" in a generic way, Sarkar introduced a Sanskrit concept called "vrtti," meaning tendency or propensity. When referring to general human expressions Sarkar preferred the terms "vrttis" or "propensities". He used "emotion" to represent an expression that was instinctive in an individual's personality. The concept of vrtti or propensity originally hails from eastern esoteric philosophy that divides all human expressions into fifty primary groupings. Each grouping ranges from a low to a high intensity. For instance, one grouping is the tendency (or vrtti) related to feeling helpless. This covers a range of expression such as insecure, overwhelmed, trapped, hopeless, and defeated.

Everyone manifests the fifty groupings of human tendencies both internally and externally. To illustrate, the expression of shame can be internally or externally displayed. A man experiences shame inside while no one else knows or he outwardly indicates it through different sensory and motor organs such as walking with a bowed head or being so disconcerted he becomes tongue tied. All together, people have over a thousand arrays of expression. This calculation comes from taking the fifty human tendencies and multiplying them by two, representing their internal or external manifestations. The resultant is a hundred tendencies, which use the ten sensory and motor organs as their medium for expression. By multiplying one hundred tendencies with ten, for the ten organs, the result is one thousand expressions. Esoteric art portrays this as a lotus flower with a thousand petals sitting at the top of the head like a crown. The following list consists of Sarkar's fifty groupings of human tendencies.[30]

FOUR BASIC LONGINGS
- physical longings
- psychic longings
- psycho-spiritual longings
- spiritual longings

SIX MUNDANE ATTITUDES
- indifference
- lack of common sense
- over indulgence
- lack of confidence
- hopelessness
- crude manners

TEN VISCERAL DRIVES
- shyness
- sadistic tendency
- envy
- inertia
- melancholia
- peevishness
- yearning for acquisition
- blind attachment
- hatred
- fear

TWELVE TRIGGERS
- hope
- deep thinking
- effort
- love
- arrogance
- discernment
- psychic depression

- conceit
- avarice
- hypocrisy
- argumentative
- repentance

SIXTEEN HIGHER QUALITIES
- tendency inspired by first musical note
- tendency inspired by second musical note
- tendency inspired by third musical note
- tendency inspired by fourth musical note
- tendency inspired by fifth musical note
- tendency inspired by sixth musical note
- tendency inspired by seventh musical note
- tendency aroused from creation (om)
- tendency aroused by divine current (kundalini)
- fruition
- mundane advancement
- welfare in subtler sphere
- pious resolve
- spiritual surrender
- repulsion
- attraction

TWO TRAITS OF MASTERY
- understanding mundane knowledge
- understanding spiritual knowledge

"REACTIVE MOMENTA"

Various events and experiences cause different tendencies to be expressed. Any occurrence that creates a vivid impression, an emotional reaction, or a strong desire molds a person. For example, Bob as a young boy fell from the roof of a house and broke his arm.

His arm healed over time but the violent fall made him afraid of heights. Even as an adult, Bob kept this emotional scar. Similar to intense experiences, strong wants such as the desire for revenge can also change and mar lives. Generally, people quickly try to act upon their desires. When a desire is not met, it awaits expression. This "waiting" or dormant mode is called "reactive momentum." Usually, people have so many desires that the majority of them become subconscious. Similar to the Biblical phrase, "As you sow, you shall reap." Waiting to reap is called "reactive momenta." Reactive momenta propel people in directions favorable to the fulfillment of their subconscious desires.

When a traumatic event occurs or insignificant incidents happen very frequently, those types of experiences cause strong reactions or desires. For instance, if children frequently do not receive the full attention of their teacher, over time they may develop less esteem. They become less eager to answer their teacher's questions. Overtime, this can develop into a behavioral pattern. Frequently repeated behavior patterns become part of an individual's nature. Without realizing it, people feel, think, and act according to patterns that they subconsciously develop over time. This explains why humans act in certain ways and why specific tendencies such as fear, shame, or shyness dominate in certain people. Especially relevant are those tendencies and patterns children acquire from their home environment. Family relationships particularly are significant in making up a person's personality during the formative years. What occurs in the family and school life of young children form their patterns for life.

HELPING CHILDREN UNDERSTAND THEIR TENDENCIES

Emotional guidance or control over emotional tendencies is a significant part of morality. Moral guidance of children needs to include the development of control over the various propensities and thereby arouse their refined qualities. When children make effort toward self-control, they acquire moral strength. Additionally, they awaken higher qualities. It is very sensitive work to guide a young child in their emotional control. Teachers model and encourage good qualities and behavior patterns. Yet, when teachers observe an unhealthy behavior pattern, they can intervene to help children alter the pattern.

To guide children in the control of their various tendencies, the teacher has to be keenly aware of how young children feel. A teacher has to be sensitive and responsive to children's individual requirements and feelings. Teachers, for instance, begin their efforts from the first day of school when new children show distress at separating from their parents. By helping children to feel safer and by showing kindness, a great deal of the children's distress is alleviated. Generally, distress characterizes the most severe negative manifestation that young children display and should be taken seriously by teachers. Failure to remove a child's distress harms emotional growth. Not removing a child's distress precipitates the child's subconscious belief that the world is not a safe place. In this type of situation, the child has more difficulty advancing in moral integrity.

Another common expression of children involves the manifestation of surprise. Continuously they come upon new experiences that startle them. If most of the surprises that children experience give them pleasure, they look positively towards changes. If children perceive these surprises as negative, new changes may cause defensive behavior and other complications. There especially should not be shameful experiences that erode a child's self-worth.

Anger is just as common as surprise in children. This tendency occurs when children are restrained from an activity, interrupted, or forced to do something against their will. A good teacher often sees it coming upon children before they fully express it, and the teacher diffuses the situation. When children already appear angry, they require ways to channel or release it. Children must learn that anger is natural but that it demands an appropriate response. They have to sense it, name it, and channel it. Initially, this means teaching children to recognize the little signs of anger such as faster breathing and the tightening in the chest and other muscles. Then they name it, calling the feeling "anger." The ability to put a feeling into words makes up a huge factor in the diffusing of it. When children cannot name to themselves and to others an experience, they feel more out of control and reactionary. By calling for children "to use their words," it allows them to operate in a verbal way that does not hurt others, instead of physical ways. Additionally, children need techniques to diminish anger such as walking away, sitting aside to calm down, or seeking help from an adult who will talk them into a calmer state. Empowering children through self-awareness and by giving them the knowledge of how to turn negative experiences into positive ones gives children valuable tools needed to build a successful life.

Learning to control their tendencies and emotions helps children to value their interactions and to grow morally. When children learn control over the tendencies, they arouse refined qualities such as patience, introspection, and conviction, which lead to real moral development. The importance of this process in young children goes far beyond the experience of many individual incidents, as what happens to young children forms patterns that make up their character for life. It takes great intervention in adult life to change patterns learned in early childhood. With so much at stake, an educator understands that morality and related areas such as emotional control form the most important aspects of the curriculum. As P. R. Sarkar said,

> "That which provides the emotional ideal of the mind with inspiration to reach that cosmic stance is what we call moralism. Every aspect of this moralism goes on singing for humanity the song of the infinite in the midst of microcosm. In other words the good faculties that establish one in the cosmic state, are the very ones that constitute the virtuous principles of moralism."[31]

CAN I PLAY WITH YOU?

> *"Human civilization is like a bouquet of flowers*
> *from many different gardens –*
> *And the bouquet of these varied flowers is more*
> *beautiful*
> *Than the individual flowers themselves."*[32]
>
> Sarkar

Neo-humanism attributes to ethics the importance of being the anchor for social progress. Ethics and social skills give a future gauge of success, more than do academic subjects. For instance, upon maturity children may be bright, but without good ethics and socialization skills, they may not have as much success or happiness. Neo-humanists educators regard role modeling as one of the critical ways children learn ethics and good social skills. The adult's role is paramount for children to observe.

Social growth as an extension of moral development, refers to the following ethical principles: non-harming, benevolent truthfulness, non-stealing, universal love, simple living, and service. Children express these principles in their lives by learning to play cooperatively. They learn how to give and take. They make friends and develop empathy towards others and even towards inanimate objects. Learning ethics is a subtle process that entails children's examining beliefs about themselves and others. Do children believe they are worthy people with important contributions to make? Do their smiles brighten the day, or are they ignored and scorned? If trust has been offered to children, they become trusting and open.

If young children have felt neglected or have been ignored, for example, not fed when hungry or not comforted when distressed, they feels weaker and less valuable in their relationships.

Most educators agree that ethical and social development is significantly tied to other areas of children's development. Learning is very integrated, like a delicately woven tapestry, each thread enhancing another. For instance, while children learn language, they may also improve morality and social skills indirectly. In this way, Neo-humanist educators look at most of children's experiences as integrated, especially ethical, emotional, and social opportunities.

PSYCHO-SOCIAL STAGES

To facilitate children in creating harmonious social relations, particular care is given in the early childhood years. From this critical developmental period, the way children mature will have ramifications throughout life. During the early years, social maturation unfolds in a complicated process of predictable learning stages. Many theories explain the various stages a child goes through in social growth. Cognitive psychologist Erik Erickson focused on what he called "psycho-social" stages of development. He believed that all people go through certain developmental stages throughout their lives. At each stage individuals meet dilemmas they must resolve or tests they have to complete. Any stage that is not successfully completed leaves a residue that effects all subsequent stages. Erickson believed that children's success in completing a stage is heavily dependent on their relationships with their significant adults.

Each of Erickson's developmental stages centers on a specific core value. At each stage a child would either learn a specific value or its opposite, the results becoming integrated into the child's personality. For instance, if children do not acquire trust as infants, they evolve distrust instead. This forms a negative subconscious pattern of distrust throughout adult life. Usually, this pattern would remain and affect the person throughout life or until something else significantly changed it.

When a core personality element such as trust remains unrealized, the phenomenon is called "arrested development." Arrested development refers to a break in an individual's healthy and natural development, leaving a less healthy condition that keeps driving the individual. Distrust that occurred when one was an infant colors the child's view of the world. This weakness continues until some positive intervention transpires that corrects the weakness and changes the unhealthy subconscious pattern. A positive intervention in the case of mistrust would be a significant and extended experience of trust.

In another case, due to unhealthy sibling rivalry where parents show disinterest or favoritism, a child can form begrudged sharing. The child may have an arrested development in sharing that carries on into adulthood. For instance, Arthur had parents who fought with each other and pitted the children against one another. They used the children's toys as tools in their arguments, taking away toys of children sided with the other parent and allowing "favorite" children to play with the toys they wanted. Consequently, Arthur became defensive and possessive of his toys. His childhood experience did not enable Arthur to learn to share willingly. After he grew up, without fully understanding why, Arthur felt irritable and angry whenever anyone asked to borrow his things. Even with his wife, he divided their possessions into "hers and his" instead of "ours." These feelings that drove Arthur's behavior came from arrested development in the early years. With proper re-education he may become aware of his behavior patterns and learn how to negotiate and share willingly. According to Erickson, the critical stages cover:

BIRTH TO ONE YEAR
- Basic Trust / Basic Mistrust
- I can depend on you / I can't depend on you.
- This is a safe place / I'm not safe here.

ONE TO THREE YEARS
- Autonomy / Doubt
- I can do it myself / I probably can't do it.
- You approve of me / You don't approve of me.

THREE TO FIVE YEARS
- Initiative / Guilt
- I can solve problems / I'm doing it wrong.
- I can take risks and make mistakes / I'd better not try or make mistakes.

SIX TO TEN YEARS
- Industry / Inferiority
- I find accomplishments and interests / I can't do anything right.
- There is purpose / Life is boring.

ELEVEN TO SEVENTEEN YEARS
- Identity / Confusion when assuming different roles
- Strives to know "Who am I?" / Is reactive, rebellious and promiscuous.
- Authentic / Acts one way to parents and another way to others

EIGHTEEN TO THIRTY-NINE YEARS
- Intimacy / Isolation
- I am responsible / I lack stability and have trouble with intimacy.
- Shares and affiliates with others / Needs to control or be controlled.

FORTY TO SIXTY-FOUR YEARS
- Contribution / Stagnation
- Leadership / Self-absorbed

SIXTY-FIVE ON
- Integrity / Despair
- Great counsel / Regrets and bitterness[33]

ROLE MODELING

A teacher can intervene with a troubled child by providing consistent help and love at school. Children learn a tremendous amount through their teacher's example. If they see the teacher modeling concern for others, fairness, and co-operating with others, the children will tend towards these themselves. Positive, consistent modeling goes a long way in motivating a child to adopt good behavior and to seek help when needed.

Occasionally, times arise when children lose control or have negative feelings, and need redirecting. In cases of children who often display negative behavior, they usually have low self-esteem and arrested development. These children demand much reassurance and good, consistent guidance. For instance a boy who pushes another child in front of the teacher for no apparent reason. When he exhibits negative behavior to attract attention, his teacher helps by not rejecting him and by channeling him towards more positive beliefs about himself. By focusing on the positive instead of the negative, children learn both self-worth and self-control. The core social beliefs such as "I am worthy" or "My contributions count" become the auto-pilot of the child's life. Certainly these efforts are at the heart of teaching morality and at guiding young children socially. With appropriate and consistent care, a teacher furthers children's self images and social patterns. These images and patterns may drive children their entire life.

Good role models are essential for early growth. Children gain social ethics and social skills through authentic role models and through the rewarding of efforts in an open and empathetic atmosphere. Ethics and social skills can never be acquired by rote memory or by force. In the spirit of play, children learn social ethics and social skills.

STAGES OF PLAY

Other stages related to children's social development are from the work of renowned cognitive psychologist Jean Piaget, who described children's stages of play. Social development, similar to other areas of development, primarily takes place in the arena of play. In play children first relate to the world about them. Teachers observe children go set stages of social play regardless of their intelligence or cultural backgrounds. Before two years of age, most children primarily play by themselves. Usually then around two to three years old, children take interest in what other children do. They play along side other children, parallel to them. For instance, a little girl starts building a blockhouse and a two-year old boy sees her and comes over. He will start his own instead of joining her. With maturity, in little phases, they gradually increase their play with other children. Around three or four years of age, children generally begin the group play stage and interact with other children. This becomes more sophisticated with age and experience. Exposing children to playmates at younger ages through nursery programs advance these skills sooner. Likewise, children who do not have many social opportunities to play with other children learn these stages later.

Early play stages critically influence the evolution of character. Teachers and parents have to give children a positive atmosphere for character and social development. During these young ages, the character patterns they form usually remain for life. Any arrested development that occurs affects a child's future growth. A child can have arrested development due to traumatic experiences, continuous rejections, or a frequent lack of success over time. For instance, if arrested development occurs in a toddler when he is learning to respect other children's boundaries, that individual may keep elements of being inconsiderate of others throughout his life. It takes a huge change as an adult to break a personality pattern that occurs during early years.

PROMOTING SOCIAL SKILLS

For children to have good social skills they need to also have good role models that demonstrate kindness and care. Without a sense of being loved and cared for, a child has no motivation to acquire socially oriented moral concepts and skills. When children feel acceptance and security, they more likely form positive feelings about themselves and others. For instance, self-assured children have an easier time in the early stages of sharing. A stronger sense of self engenders them with a resilient base, not easily crushed by the process of trial and error.

Many activities help a child flourish in their interactions with others. Dramatic play constitutes one of the best activities for young children as they naturally are inclined to play at imitating the world. In this type of play they practice getting along with others. Teaches can organize a special corner for "dress ups" to facilitate dramatic play. This corner could include child-sized furniture, dolls, dishes, and used adult clothes. Dramatic corners can change to fit various themes such as a restaurant, an office, or a beauty parlor. By rotating the props in the drama corner around certain themes, the teacher not only aids social development, but also cognitive skills and language growth. Dressing up and pretending to be someone else provides invaluable experiences in understanding different roles.

Any small group activity where children have to co-operate and share with others supports social development. Good group activities such as group art projects and science experiments provide opportunities for problem solving and give children a sense of belonging. Block play is another excellent way to aid social skills. Block play allows children to naturally progress through the different stages of play – solitary play, parallel play, and group play. In block building with other children, the group makes a plan, discusses its progress, decides on the final use, and when and how the structure is to be knocked down. This requires the children to co-operate and negotiate. Block-play also advances language and spatial awareness. Most group play contributes vital information to children about their value to others and about life.

SERVICE SPIRIT

As part of social development, Neo-humanist education includes the responsibility to serve others. From their earliest years, teachers nurture children's service spirit. Service is an essential Neo-humanist concept. When social skills blossom into service awareness, that is the highest fulfillment. Service touches the hearts of others more than other kinds of interactions. Society attributes greatness to a person's actions and not to a person's intentions. By pointing out opportunities as they arise or by creating opportunities for children to do service, teachers help young children develop more awareness of it. Cleaning the school yard, making get well cards for sick classmates, thank you cards for visitors, and singing songs to old folks are some activities that children can undertake to feel the experience of service.

Service is not done for praise. It involves a genuine concern and response to another's need. Although praise is not the goal, in young children praise for service helps them learn more about its value. When children receive praise for service, they become more aware of its value and may incorporate it into their characters.

SOCIAL CONSCIENCE

Similar to service, social skills reach a higher level when there is the development of social conscience. Social development needs to be expanded to its fullest. Social conscience, linked to service, is particularly essential in Neo-humanism. Schools want to broaden children's outlook until they reach the heights of social conscience. Children need to feel a greater responsibility toward the whole world. By forming this awareness in very young children an impression is made that will be carried throughout life. In Neo-humanism the term "conscience" refers to the inner perception of a personal situation, and the term "awakened conscience" or "social consciousness" refers to understanding more distant and less subjective situations. To develop an "awakened conscience" in children, teachers need to first awaken the child's conscience and then encourage them to extend this awareness to the impersonal.

As explained in an earlier chapter, teachers promote young children's awareness of their conscience by teaching them to recognize their "uh-oh" and "ah" feelings. Children can understand the "uh-oh" and "ah" feelings as the moral sense within them when they daily interact with others. When they play and act unfairly they feel "uh-oh" and when they play nicely and help others they experience "ah" feelings. The "uh-oh" and "ah" feelings assist children in the practice of fairness, evolving in their play. These feelings teach them how to balance their individual needs and wishes with those of other children.

The development of social conscience goes beyond twinges of consciousness and involves the development of rationality. Rationality forms when children study facts and ponder pros and cons. After weighing consequences, teachers encourage children to reach decisions or judgments about the subject studied. They explain to children that the true test of a decision consists of whether the outcome benefits and does no harm to people, plants, and things. The real litmus test of a new idea is whether its outcome is universally beneficial. Neo-humanism terms this measuring stick of welfare for all an "awakened conscience." For instance, in June's class the children prepared lemonade. After discussing the ingredients the June asked the children what would happen if they put too much lemon or too little? They made a simple recipe together. When in agreement on the amounts, children prepared the drink. June extended this activity to help develop their social conscience. She asked, "We can pour a few large glasses for only a few children to drink or we can pour enough small glasses for all to drink. What should we do?" Easily the children said they wanted many small glasses so everyone could drink. This opportunity allows children to weigh consequences and decide in favor of a socially fair situation. Ask children "Is it nice to include and share with everyone?" Such discussions further the development of a social conscience.

In general, teachers find that careful attention to children's concerns about fairness reveals many teachable moments to assist children with the development of a social conscience. Most activities that promote teamwork provide opportunities to learn fairness. A collaborative learning style and one not overly competitive offers the best atmosphere for children to learn how to work with others and to develop the spirit of social equality.

Other opportunities to promote social conscience arise throughout the school year during discussion time of various themes. Teachers include questions that encourage a sense of social justice in children. From preschoolers up, teachers ask provocative questions such as should people dump garbage on the moon? Should anyone be able to own a cloud? Should anyone die for lack of water to drink because of drought? Once the children catch the idea, teachers carefully avoid teacher-child mechanistic question and response by encouraging whole-group dialogues. During the process, educators remember to thank children for their remarks and contributions.

Overall, it cannot be stated enough that children learn by observing adults. Children closely watch even the most unconscious actions of adults. By observing if teachers act fairly in their treatment of others, students pick up any bias that teachers hold. Children perceive if teachers discriminate in any way. If children are taught by example, not only to empathize with other people but with the environment as well, they become more responsible. When teachers seek out dialogues and moments to connect and aim children towards critical thinking and empathy, they go far in promoting social conscience. The development of an awakened conscience supports the children in making more astute choices and in creating solutions. When they grow up, this ability will allow them to find new solutions to alleviate human suffering.

Social development is an ethical process whose seeds are the skills of how to get along with others and whose blooms are the flowers of service and social conscience. Social conscience is a key element of Neo-humanism. As Sarkar said,

> "Remember that no created being in this universe is independent by itself – it cannot exist all by itself. All of us have a supra-cosmic relation with the rest, at times prominent, elsewhere indistinguishable. In this plan of mutual relationship, even the slightest mistake or discord anywhere will raise a furor in the universe. In this mighty task of creation the brilliantly luminous sun and insignificant ant hold the same importance of existence, all these having combined to create the world family. In the same way, in human society, as well, the importance of a highly powerful and eminent person is at par with that of a disabled or dying patient. None can be ignored. The slightest injustice done to anyone will cause the breakdown of our entire social framework."[34]

BECOMING A GUIDING STAR

"The morning glory which blooms for an hour
Differs not at heart from the giant pine,
Which lives for a thousand years."
Zen Poem

Neo-humanism upholds universality as a central concept, and this concept influences education in different ways. For instance, Universalism encourages teachers to be eclectic in developing children's learning strategies. Many past education systems collapsed due to their inability to grow and expand. In Neo-humanism, the fundamental tenets remain timeless, but ways of implementing them, of bringing ideas down to practical methods, depend on an eclectic and an evolving effort.

Guiding children and managing their behavior are two areas of education that require resourcefulness. As the field of psychology grows, newer ideas and strategies emerge to help educators guide young children. Neo-humanist teachers keep learning better ways to guide young children. They wear many "hats"; teachers have many roles. Behavioral management is often the most difficult hat to wear. Guiding children's behavior, turning their negative acts into positive experiences, can seem as perplexing as pulling a rabbit out of a magician's hat. Yet there exist simple, clear elements that a teacher can implement to become an effective counselor for young children.

BEING POSITIVE

A teacher's positive behavior endures as the single, most significant element of good guidance. One cannot underestimate a positive attitude. For instance, there was a study in Iowa by graduate students where they observed normal two-year-olds in activities throughout a day. They observed that two year olds were told what not to do four hundred and thirty-two times, as opposed to thirty-two positive acknowledgements. The national average of parent-to-child criticisms is twelve to one – that is, twelve criticisms to one compliment. Within the average secondary school classroom, the ratio of criticism to compliment is eighteen to one between teacher and student.[35]

There exists a rule of thumb stating that "for every negative statement give two positive statements," which means an average toddler in the above study would require positive reinforcing more than eight hundred times a day! A much simpler method that requires less effort than counteracting negative comments with positive ones is to have educators phrase their statements to children using more positive phrasing. They change directives such as "Take your feet off the table" to "The table is for our hands." "Don't run" becomes "Use your walking shoes." "Don't throw sand" can be phrased as "Keep the sand in the sand box." "Don't hit" becomes "Use your gentle hands". In other words, teachers positively charge the atmosphere with encouraging words, thoughts and feelings.

PRAISE AND ENCOURAGEMENT

Other common forms of positive statements consist of praise and encouragement. Teachers apply praise and positive words to children when emphasizing their good behavior. When children display appropriate and pro-social behavior, teachers commend them. "Thank you for being helpful and patient." "You were very mindful, not spilling a single drop." While this type of praise engenders children with an incentive to learn more values, it also increases a pleasant atmosphere and lets the children know the teacher cares. Young children learn virtues when they receive compliments while doing good deeds. If children exhibit empathy, the teacher says to them, "You were very understanding." When a child passes out papers, the instructor thanks the child for being helpful. When teachers reinforce through praise good behavior at the time of occurrence, children learn these virtues and appreciate the positive atmosphere.

Children appreciate praise when they show pro-social behavior such as patience, caring, and honesty. Complimenting children's finished product, on the other hand, may not serve children as well. Teachers' praise of their finished work often does not accurately reflect the way children perceive their work. It can leave children wondering why at times teachers say their work is "excellent" and at other occasions they say only "nice." Praising children's finished work is less effective than encouragement. Generally, encouragement focuses on children's work effort. Children appreciate phrases that encourage, focused on their effort, not their results. "You worked hard on that." "I saw you take your time to do it well." "Your hand must tingle from all that writing you did." Basically, the teacher uses more encouragement about a child's work and uses more praise when guiding children's behavior.

Asides from praising their conduct and encouraging their efforts in work, teachers reinforce children by other means such as quick hugs and pats, positive facial expressions, granting special privileges, and allowing independence. Physical reinforcements for small children go along way. Quick hugs and pats and positive facial expressions such as smiles move a little child along. They let the child know the teacher cares and notices them. The younger children thrive on physical pats and hugs, but the older children require less physical contact. They notice their teacher's tone of voice and body language, and they appreciate a quick pat on the shoulder. The older the child, the more the adult considers their comfort zone when giving any physical reinforcement.

RESPECT AND LOVE

Neo-humanist teachers enjoy the expression of respect and love for others. A key tenet of Neo-humanism is respect and love for every creature. With this outlook, an educator touches the perennial source of inspiration. When teachers place no limits on their loving attitudes, they feel greater flows of it. In their work, with their students, they express more love as well. As Neo-humanists, they base their attraction on seeing each child as a manifestation of Infinite Consciousness. Their principles guide them, not their instincts.

Good educators have warm glows in their hearts for the children and the children perceive it. When children feel valued, their self-images grow. They are more open to learning. For instance, when children believe they are unlovable, children may do negative behavior to prove it. Actually, children are testing what limits teachers have before they become "unloved." Such children want teachers to provide them safer boundaries, closer watching, and reassuring love. Teachers explain to their students that even if reprimands are sometimes necessary, they still care.

A child's negative behavior could turn away a teacher who is not pledged to caring for children in a loving manner. This commitment reminds the teacher to pursue greater depths of understanding regarding to what is occurring. It may take more training to understand it fully, but the teacher will help the process with warmth and commitment. Devoted teachers welcome and appreciate the love they naturally feel, and they express it and enhance it through training. As Sarkar said:

> "The teacher must bear in mind that whatever be the ages of his students - child, teenager, youth, or old person - all

are but children of different ages, and he, too, is a child like them.... In absence of this mutual affection, the free and proper exchange of ideas will be simply impossible."[36]

TEACHER AS A COUNSELOR

Educators continuously update their knowledge in child development and child psychology to improve their strategies of guidance and behavioral management. Frankly, there seems a never-ending amount to learn. Generally, teaching happy children takes the same guidance strategy as working with troubled children, only the latter require more patience. Upset children and children with low esteem, often demand attention by repeatedly exhibiting negative behavior. It falls to the teachers to investigate what is going on at home. The teacher has to also determine what the child perceives is occurring at school. In a sense, teachers have to fill a role of both teacher and counselor. At first this task may seem too great or "beyond the job description," yet it still falls on the teachers' shoulders. The class exists like a little family, part of the universal family, and educators act as the guiding force. In this position educators carry the responsibility to do their utmost for each child, especially in difficult cases. Troubled children face difficult situations, and teachers cannot ignore, turn their backs, or hand them over to someone else. Good character and spiritual life gives the educators the strength to reach deeper within them to help all the children in their care. Children look to see if teachers reach out to every child. By giving more attention to a troubled child, teachers reassure other children that everyone gets what they need, especially in a crisis.

Each educator adopts an effective and appropriate system to support children in their trials and efforts. The educators direct children toward better behavior and let the children feel accepted. One of the best systems incorporates methods such as mirroring, validating, empathy, and giving consequences.

Mirroring is a technique the teacher uses where they repeat or paraphrase whatever students say after students speak. For instance, Tim wanted to play with Jordan, but Jordan was already happily playing with Carol. Tim hit and pushed Jordan when he told him that he could not play. When the teacher asked Tim what caused him to hit Jordan, he said, "I hit him because he was not my friend." The teacher paraphrased, "You hit him because he said he was not your friend." "Does that mean you hit Jordan because he would not play with you." Tim shook his head yes and his body sighed. The teacher utilized mirroring to find out what occurred, what the child believed happened, and the child's viewpoint. Mirroring is repeating back without judgment what the child says. It forms an essential part of a process that enables a child to feel empowered and heard. Often children open up and talk more when teachers use mirroring.

After mirroring, teachers validate children by saying that they see their point or reason; for instance, "By hitting Jordan, I can see how you made your point to him how you did not like that he did not play with you." "Tim shook his head yes. Validating does not mean approval of the behavior, but it acknowledges that the child had a reason, regardless of what it was. Children who have weak characters usually lack validation by the significant adults in their life. Repeated negative-behavior-seeking in many cases becomes a cry for validation. The process of validation trusts that every action has a purpose, regardless of whether it comes from a good choice or not.

After children know they are validated, teachers focus on the feelings involved; for instance the children's anger or fear. By introducing empathy into the scenario of hitting, teachers assure children that they understand how they feel. They help children how the other the child, the victim, feels. "I know you were angry with Jordan. But you hurt him when you hit him and made him feel unhappy." In the guidance process, using empathy proceeds giving a consequence as it reassures the child that you do understand their feelings. Validation was the acknowledgment of their motivation, whereas empathy focuses on the feelings involved.

At the end of guidance comes the process of explaining and giving consequences. The teacher asked Tim, "What else could you do instead of hitting Jordan to show him you did not like him not playing with you?" Tim said, "I could have told teacher." The teacher answered, "Yes you can ask teacher to help you, but what else could you do? Can you tell Jordan how you feel?" Next time tell Jordan, "I am not happy that I cannot play. But we can play later." By doing that Jordan knows how you feel but you let him know you want to play later. Then the teacher had Tim practice saying it. After that she told Tim he still needed a consequence for hurting Jordan and he was "timed out". One of the best consequences for young children is called "time out" or "calming down time." "Time out" consists of asking the child to sit at the side of the play area for a short duration to calm down and reflect. In this consequence, non-participation is the punishment and participation is the reward. The duration of how long a child stays on "time out" goes according to age. The rule of thumb is one minute per year of life. For instance, Tim is a four-year-old and receives a four-minute "time out" period. "Time out" does not mean moving children to a specific corner or a chair designated only for punishments. Rather, teachers give "time out" in the same spirit as referees in a sports game; it means sitting conveniently to the side of the activity. Teachers want to create an atmosphere of fairness, not embarrassment or strictness.

After "time out" finishes, and especially if someone was "timed out" due to hurting another child, the teacher follows it up with asking the child to go and say, "Are you OK?" to the hurt child. In the past, teachers customarily forced children to apologize and say, "I'm sorry," which often caused a begrudged or forced response. The empathetic "Are you OK?" perfectly opens a bridge to the child without the other child losing self-esteem in the process. Rarely children refuse this simple offer to reach out to their "victims", whereas apologizing may seem too much for some children. Additionally it offers the development of empathy. For instance, Jill hit her friend at the puzzle table and the teacher after dialoguing with her gave a "time out". She said, "You are on "time out" for hitting your friend because hitting hurts." The teacher asked Jill to sit at the side of the room near, but not at, the puzzle-table. Before letting Jill rejoin the play the teacher asked her, "Can you hear the little voice in your heart saying, "uh-oh" when you hit your friend?" Jill shakes her head no. Teacher tells Jill to take a deep breath and calm down so she can hear or feel it. Then she asks, "Can you ask your friend if she is OK?" Jill shook her head yes and went up to her friend, saying "Are you OK?" Her friend shook her head yes and promptly told Jill she could play with her again.

During class time, teachers encourage children to use their words with their friends, often giving simple prompting. They can empower children by teaching children how to use basic phrases such as "I want to play." "I do not like that." "Can I play?" "I will play with you later." "Can I have a turn?" "Will you let me join?" "Stop, that." If children express their desires in words, conflicts soon become more manageable to solve. Children learn that words hold tremendous power and that words complement play.

When a teacher uses the process of mirroring, validation, empathy, and giving consequences, children feel open for more guidance because they unconsciously appreciate the psychological effect of the process. Ordinary teacher-child interactions thus transform into more ethical ones. Within the structure of these systematic and calm child-teacher dialogues, acceptance and promotion of good values will begin to underlay morality. This systematic approach puts morality into action for the children to experience.

The process of mirroring, validation, empathy, and giving consequences is very universal as these skills cover disruptive behavior, distressful moments, and social conflicts. Further the skills facilitate trust, communication, and help minimize distress as well. In penetrating meetings, usually new insights and deeper feelings surface about what children think and feel, and the teacher can help by validating and giving them affection. To illustrate, a teacher wants to soothe a distressed boy named Joshua who misses his working mother. The same system for disciplining helps the teacher know what to say to comfort the child. She said Joshua, "Do you miss your mother?" He cried and said he did. "I understand that you love your Mom and want to be with her more. I know you miss her and you feel a little scared when you're away from her." said the teacher. Next she reassured Joshua that his mother would pick him up later, "Mother wants you to go to school and make friends. She will pick you up in a little while. I will help you and protect you while Mom is away." At this point the teacher gave him a hug, held his hand and walked amongst the other children.

A proper guidance system, in the hands of a kind teacher, is similar to rare pearls. The teacher offers a unique pearl of wisdom to each child. Over time the pearls will accumulate and turn into a strand that all appreciate. The same guidance process of mirroring, validation, empathy, and giving consequences works for all students yet in its application perfectly adjusts to each situation. The teacher will blossom into a wonderful guide. Long ago philosopher Goethe said, "If you treat an individual . . . as if he were what he ought to be and could be, he will become what he ought to be and could be."

WHAT I WANT TO KNOW IS?

> *"It is in fact short of a miracle that the modern methods of instructions*
> *Have not yet entirely strangled the holy curiosity of inquiry for these delicate little plants;*
> *Aside from stimulations, they stand mainly in need of freedom.*
> *Without this, it goes to wrack and ruin."*[36]
>
> Einstein

Understanding how children physically mature and evolve their cognitive abilities is crucial knowledge for an educator. Although much research still goes on in this field, educators remain at the beginning of their understanding. Recent studies suggest that children create their own knowledge; children use the physical and mental tools they are born with to explore their environment. As children make sense of their environment, they construct their own mental images. The belief that children create their own knowledge has existed since long ago, although it is recently being scientifically researched. Philosopher, Swami Vivekananda said in the 1800's,

> "All knowledge that the world has ever received comes from the mind; the infinite library of the universe is in your own mind. The external world is simply the suggestion, the occasion, which sets you to study your own mind, but the object of your study is always your own mind. The

falling of an apple gave the suggestion to Newton, and he studied his own mind; he re-arranged all the previous links of thought in his mind and discovered a new link among them, which we call the law of gravitation. It was not in the apple nor in anything in the center of the earth."[37]

Present scientific research suggests the brain, in predictable patterns, organizes the child's knowledge from birth. Most educators believe that children inherit some of these patterns, while other patterns result from childhood explorations. Scientists and educators believe that children go through universal developmental stages in cognitive growth. Children may vary when and how quickly they go through each stage, but they all mature through progressive sequences. Regardless of the child's culture or intelligence, these steps occur. Children's genetic makeup and environment influence the ease and richness of their development through these stages.

ROLE OF PLAY

What vital aspects of cognitive development does Sarkar stress for Neo-humanist educators? Foremost, he believed that young children create their knowledge through play, that the principle direction of sense exploration and play in young children is learning. Far beyond recreation, play makes up the way children experiment and discover. As P. R. Sarkar said, "Children are inclined towards play, so the thirst for knowledge in children can be awakened through the medium of play. And through this alone children may be taught."[38]

Teachers know young children play using their senses (perceptual learning). Driven by a strong inner urge, they want to touch, feel, manipulate, and hold everything within reach. This invokes their natural curiosity and requires encouragement. These natural urges can be supported or hindered by the environment and adults. The psychological and physical environment has to enable children to playfully explore through their motor and sense organs while adults convey messages of approval. If the surroundings seem uninteresting or the caregivers too controlling or neglectful, they may not evolve their intellect. For instance, Stephen Glenn, a famous scientist who made several important medical breakthroughs, explained to reporters his creativity came from an experience with his mother at two years old.

> While removing a bottle of milk from the refrigerator he dropped and spilled it. Instead of punishing him, his mother said, "Robert, what a great and wonderful mess you have made! I have rarely seen such a huge puddle of milk. Well, the damage has already been done. Would you like to get down and play in the milk for a few minutes before we clean it up?"
>
> Indeed he did. After a few minutes, his mother said, "You know, Robert, whenever you make a mess like this, eventually you have to clean it up and restore everything to its proper order. So, how would you like to do that? We could use a sponge, a towel or a mop. Which do you prefer?" He chose the sponge and together they cleaned up the mess.
>
> His mother then said, "You know, what we have here is a failed experiment in how to effectively carry a big milk bottle with two tiny hands. Let's go in the back yard and fill the bottle with water and see if you can discover a way to carry it without dropping it." The little boy learned that if he grasped the bottle at the top near the lip with both hands, he could carry it without dropping it.
>
> It was at that moment that he knew he did not need to be afraid to make mistakes. Instead, he learned that mistakes were just opportunities for learning something new, which is what scientific experiments are all about."[39]

Good educators prepare activities and the environment to enhance children's cognitive play. They become play partners of their young students. Play partners watch children play and look for ways to enhance their play with suggestions and questions that encourage children to think, reason, question, and experiment. Good play partners first observe children to learn what interests them. Each child is unique and teachers notice each child's interest, stage, and learning style. Then teachers follow their children's leads and enhance and support their play. Following each child's lead sends the message that the teacher thinks the child is important and has good ideas.

AROUSE THEIR CURIOSITY

Related to play, Sarkar stresses another important concept in cognitive development, the arousal of a child's sense of curiosity and wonder.

> "The thirst for knowledge must be awakened. Developing the mind goes far beyond an understanding of math, science and language. Mere intelligence is not enough. An educator's aim is to motivate a child to desire to assimilate the entire universe."[40]

Although curiosity naturally belongs to children, before they enter school their previous experiences may either have quelled or have increased their curious natures. By listening to the type and amount of questions they ask, the teacher learns if the child avidly explores new things or shows little interest in new things. Does the child mainly ask permission questions such as "Can I have paper?" Or does the child ask why and how questions about things? For instance, "Where is my friend? Is she going to school?" "The picture in this book looks like my dog. Do you have a dog like this" Such questions make up curious and inquiring interactions. Less curious children ask few how, why, or where questions. Educators pick this up and revitalize their curiosity by their support and type of answers.

Regularly asking "open-ended" questions advances curiosity and builds thinking and problem solving skills as well. Educators call questions with many possible answers open-ended questions, contrasting them with questions that demand yes, no, or only one right answer. Teachers appreciate the various perspectives they receive from students who answer open-ended questions. Teachers should apply this important skill of questioning to all ages. Provocative questions empower a child's curiosity.

OPEN-ENDED QUESTIONS INCLUDE:
- How could we
- What else can you do with
- Where else do you suppose
- How else could you
- What if
- What can you tell me about this

CLOSED QUESTIONS INCLUDE:
- Who is your
- What do you call
- Is that
- Do you know what this is
- What is the name of
- What is it

For young children, the inclusion of many sensory questions also assists their curiosity. When possible, teachers follow the children's leads. If they do not show interest, teachers start by asking sensory questions. Does anything smell different? What else does this feel like to you? How do these objects look, sound, and feel? With assistance, children can collect data about a topic and compare and contrast it, which can lead to an activity of designing poster displays. Collecting, comparing, questioning and recording comprise important aspects of scientific thought and encourage curiosity.

If children require reawakening of their curiosity, the teacher needs to take special care to show genuine interest in things and in their interactions. When children show little curiosity, teachers exaggerate their interest in various ways to serve as a behavior model. Their enthusiasm ignites the child's interest to ask, think, and solve new concepts. For instance introducing new materials in the classroom such as seeds, eggs, gloves, and tools excite children's curiosity. Investigating these types of things engages more then one sense. The children can imagine events and other things associated around them. Regularly the staff may decide what concepts they would like to explore with the children and what new things to display.

UNIVERSAL AND FACTUAL INSTRUCTION

In addition to play and curiosity, Sarkar emphasized that children's instruction has to be based on fact and free from any narrow-mindedness. For a child to obtain his full cognitive potential, learning must be universally based. Racism, sexism, or nationalism cannot shadow instruction. Teachers carefully select books that show both genders doing a variety of roles and non-stereotypical themes. Conscientiously educators seek out books that do not favor one race over others. Unfortunately, in upper grades many of the available books slant knowledge in a direction to further a group's interests. In certain subjects it is more difficult to acquire factual and non-bias books. Major examples are history books that favor certain viewpoints and medical and health textbooks that favor interests groups such as the poultry and pharmaceutical industry. Educators are tasked with choosing books, activities, and learning events for their classrooms that maintain a factual and non-biased atmosphere.

DEVELOPING AN UNAFFECTED AND BALANCED MIND

Keeping the children's and teachers' minds free of distractions while encouraging a balanced outlook are other important aspects to cognitive development, according to Sarkar. He believed that a "fundamental of education is that teachers and students should have a balanced mind, unaffected, unassailed by unimportant entities."[41] Often unwanted, outside distraction triumphs over children's ability to learn. With today's overwhelming amount of information, only ordered and organized minds fully appreciate and use the vast knowledge available. Teachers help children learn how to focus and organize their minds.

Helping young children focus occurs through play with teachers acting as play partners. For instance, Laura, Daniel, and Jesse busily built a blockhouse. Their teacher, June, watched Daniel and Jesse place blocks to make a wall. She verbalized their play saying, "Daniel is using a large rectangular block. Now Jesse adds a small rectangular block to make the wall longer." By describing their play process, June helped the children think about what they were doing and make connections. She added new vocabulary words and mathematical concepts. Further, June saw opportunities to expand and extend the activity. June asked the block builders if they wanted to add a door and a TV antenna to their house. Laura put a small triangular shape block on top of the block wall and said it was the TV antenna. The children became excited and added other blocks to decorate their blockhouse. Teachers as play partners help children focus by following their leads, interpreting their play, and expanding and extending it.

Overall, young children's development of balanced minds, free of distractions, hinges on their ability to order knowledge and make connections. The various ways children organize and make choices metamorphoses as children progress and mature. Very young children need to learn the most fundamental ideas. Some of the most rudimentary ideas young children acquire revolve around the concepts of shapes, colors, sizes, numbers, time, and space. Cognitive psychologists, such as Jean Piaget, discovered that children evolve their basic concepts in stages. When teachers understand the sequences children go through in learning these fundamental ideas, they can more accurately assist children in successfully accomplishing each step. For instance, shapes are one of the first concepts children assimilate. In the first stage of learning shapes children think all enclosed figures are the same. A young child categorizes a circle and square as the same, as they over-generalize the shapes. As they explore the shapes they begin to see similarities and differences. They learn a house is square, but when they see a box they cannot automatically transfer the knowledge about the houses' shape to the box's shape. Separately, they learn that the box is square. After discovering separately the square shape of several items, gradually they transfer the concept to all similarly shaped objects. In this manner children learn every shape. Teachers enhance their efforts by providing children with ample opportunities to explore shapes and talk about them during their play.

Similar to understanding shapes, children learn about colors. Infants show a fascination with colors, and they can differentiate colors but do not know their names. When children begin to talk, they randomly use any color name for any color. They may call a blue ball red. Soon, they memorize a few specific things that have a certain color; for instance, they can name their shirt as red. But if shown a red card, they do not know its name. Each red they see, they believe is different. Children require much practice to generalize red to all similar things, as they do not transfer this knowledge immediately. Color games, color songs, and painting make up some of the fun activities that assist children in acquiring knowledge of colors.

Although every cognitive skill is equally valuable, educators often prioritize the learning of numbers. When children begin to learn numbers they first say the name of numbers, without understanding their meaning. Children enjoy using numbers in their speech when they receive encouragement. Overtime children understand that the spoken form of a number involves counting: "one" is for one object and "two" is for two objects. Children learn counting when they enjoy counting a variety of things such as counting beads, counting snacks at snack time, and counting fingers and toes. Parallel to these types of activities, teachers help children understand written numbers. Written numerals, being far more abstract, emerge much slower and later than counting. When children first begin to use numerals, they use them indiscriminately. This means children recognize number symbols but none have a specific meaning. They grasp that they mean something, "a 2 is not a 5," but they do not know what exactly they are. At this stage children attempt to represent different objects with different numerals at random. Finally, they gain the understanding of a single numeral and its quantity. Understanding of more numerals soon follows. While learning the meaning of numbers and their symbols, children have to feel they are playing and having fun. Each stage has to be a rich sensorial experience, exciting and worthwhile from the children's perspective.

As the fundamental cognitive concepts unfurl in a child's world, memory arises. Memory depends on classification, seriation, number, time, and space. By integrating an understanding of these concepts, memory occurs. Every new experience changes the view of previous experiences. The more rich and varied children's activities are the better. Memory has three aspects: recognition, recall, and recollection. Infants' memory busies itself with recognition. By the toddler stage, children begin to acquire the ability to recall. Recall means children no longer require an outside object to kindle memory. For example, a teacher asked David, a toddler, to find the ball that was on the shelf in the next room. He went to the shelf and found the ball because he remembered where it was. He did not have to see the ball to recall it. After recall comes recollection, the most advanced aspect of memory, and it occurs when children have the ability to group information in a meaningful way. For example, when preschool children learn various action songs, it means they can recollect each song and its actions in their memory.

Every stage of memory depends on children playing in sensorial ways. The more varied and fun the children's exploration, the more connections they will make. Children learn theses skills while they build with blocks, manipulate play dough shapes, dramatically play store, and sing number songs. When children learn in a perceptually rich and fun manner, they enjoy focusing, memorizing, and thinking.

In summary, balanced and undistracted thinking requires an orderly mind. Only an ordered and organized mind fully appreciates and uses the vast knowledge available. Very young children need to learn the most fundamental ideas such as shapes, colors, sizes, and numbers in order to organize knowledge. Because perceptual or sensory learning make up the foundation of how young children acquire these concepts, children with rich perceptual experiences develop more extensive memories and thought processes. Teachers of young children carefully help children develop these basic concepts in a richly sensorial and play-way manner. Children with vivid and varied sensory experiences will appreciate there are many ways to think and remember instead of just one.

CYCLE OF CREATION

Neo-humanism has an additional cognitive concept to organize knowledge called the "cycle of creation." To young children the "cycle of creation" starts as simple mythology that prepares their minds for philosophical and abstract thought. Cycle of creation encourages children to believe that everything has a similar origin, is connected, and is changing. Sarkar theorized the Infinite Consciousness makes up the essence of creation and explores itself in a de-evolutionary and evolutionary journey. Just as water transforms from steam to liquid to ice, and then again from ice to water to steam, depending on the temperature of its environment, yet it remains always water. Similarly, Infinite Consciousness transforms from subtle psychic forms into solidified physical forms, yet remains Infinite Consciousness.

In the first phase of the "cycle of creation", Infinite Consciousness de-evolves into the physical universe with dormant mental properties. During the second phase, life begins within certain chemical combinations as a result of physical clash. The primitive mind evolves in complexity through various stages of animal life until it reaches humanity. At the human level, people individually begin their final effort to regain the cosmic status whereby each person gradually reemerges into cosmic awareness. The complete dance of creation, from and back to Infinite Consciousness, is the cycle of creation. Human beings have the capacity to complete this cosmic cycle. Through nurturing the subtle qualities and insights of their own inner consciousness, human beings learn to recognize the one, loving Infinite Consciousness inherent in them and in the vast creation.

This underlying theme of an integral Oneness runs through all the activities and teachings at a Neo-humanistic school, providing a synthetic view of life and engendering the child with an intuitional understanding of the Cosmos. Children familiar with the cycle of creation can ponder the idea that "the movement of a single ant upon the earth reverberates in the entire Cosmos." On a day to day level, the concept of the cycle of creation helps children organize knowledge into a cohesive whole. Teachers introduce the cycle of creation in story form, in a song, and in a pictorial chart. Below is an example of the cycle of creation in a simple story form for preschoolers called, "The Circle of Love".

> First, there was only one, loving Infinite Being. The loving Infinite Being wanted someone to love, but there

was no one to love. It wanted to play, but there was no one to play. Then the Infinite Being thought, " I am going to make some playmates." So the Infinite Being began to create out of its dreams.

First it made a simple song, "OOMM, OOMM." The Infinite Being kept singing and singing that song. The song traveled everywhere and formed a vast playground, a vast space with no beginning and no end. Although the Infinite Being had a beautiful song and playground, it still felt alone and sighed. From that sigh, came the air. Wind whistled throughout the big playground of space. The Infinite Being liked the feeling of the soft wind blowing.

The beautiful song and soft wind were nice, but it was very, very dark. The Infinite Being could not see anything at all. Next it made many beautiful stars to light the darkness. With the shining light of the bright stars, the Infinite Being could see a long way. It felt happy and cried joyful tears. The happy tears made giant raindrops that flowed and filled the sea. Then the Infinite Being swam in the sea and splashed in the rolling waves. Tall mountains and little hills appeared from the sea. The Infinite Being sat on the mountain and hill tops and looked out over the water.

For a long time the Infinite Being played with the wind and the water — splashing in the streams and snoring with the sleeping rocks. Yet, the Infinite Being still felt lonely. So the earth awoke with many tiny plants. They grew in the oceans and on the land. Colorful plants covered the earth.

Still the loving, Infinite Being wanted more. It wished to watch something move and walk about more freely. Ants, butterflies, fish, frogs, and snakes came to life. Then lizards, birds, rabbits, kangaroos, and kittens began to live. There were many different colored animals with different sounds: hiss, chirp, and meow. The animals made much noise.

Even then the Infinite Being felt lonely. It wanted a special toy that could feel love and could love back. The rivers, rocks, and rhinoceroses never gave a single thought to the Infinite Being. They never thought about their creator. So the loving, Infinite Being made someone who could think and love. Someone who would help take care of this big playground and everything in it. Lovingly, it made little girls and boys. Now the Infinite Being was very happy and not lonely anymore. There were people to love and they could love back. The girls and boys wanted to be so much like the loving, Infinite Being. They knew that by loving with all their hearts they could become closer and closer, until they became one with the Infinite Being. So this story is like a Circle of Love, because it ends where it began — with the love of the Infinite Being.[42]

The Cycle of Creation influences the child to see life in a continuous process of transitions, to make connections and relationships, and to realize humans have a purpose. All rudimentary concepts, from understanding shapes and colors to grasping the Cycle of Creation, fundamentally support children's understanding of the world and provoke in them new questions. Through clear basic concepts children explore, categorize, and organize their physical and mental world developing memory and logic. These basic tools help children to have a more organized mind, less vulnerable to distractions.

SUMMARY

Sarkar has enriched Neo-humanist education with insights of how to assist children in their cognitive development. He starts with the emphasis that learning must be through play, and special care needs to be given to awakening children's curiosity. Further Sarkar stresses keeping the information taught in the class factual and universally based, free of narrowness and vested interests. Children naturally gravitate towards truth and their innocent minds rely on their teachers to present them facts. Another important effort Sarkar said should go to helping both the teachers and the children maintain uncluttered and balanced minds. He said:

> "We have to keep in view three fundamentals before imparting education. The first is that education must always be based on factuality. There must not be the injection of any dogma or fanaticism or any type of geographical or racial chauvinism in the education system. The second fundamental is that education must awaken the thirst for knowledge in the student's minds. The students themselves create environmental pressure by persistent demands for answer to queries like "What is the answer? Is it correct?" The longing, "I wish to know. I wish to understand and assimilate the entire universe." should be created. The third fundamental of education is that teachers and students should have balanced minds, unaffected, unassailed by unimportant entities."[43]

WRITING IS AS NATURAL AS HOLDING A SPOON

> *"Little flower – but if I could understand*
> *What you are, root and all, and all in all*
> *I should know what God and (child) is."*[44]
> *Alfred Lord Tennyson*

Great poetry begins with the ABC's in early childhood, and proper encouragement in these early years makes a profound difference. For people new to teaching young children, it may come as a surprise that the learning process for understanding writing and reading parallels the way children learn numbers and other cognitive skills. Similar to numbers, literacy unfolds in progressive stages. For Sarkar, the need for sensorial play, curiosity, focus, and the desire to find meaning are essential elements to literacy. He understood learning to speak, read, and write emerges in children's own time as an outcome of playfully exploring with proper guidance from adults. Simply put, through well-guided play children discover literacy. Literacy is as natural and inside children as learning to walk and holding a spoon.

There are various approaches to help children learn writing and reading. Some approaches may work particularly well for certain learning styles. Overall there are key elements to keep in mind when teaching children literacy. Children want to speak, write, and read and this knowledge lies inside them. Actually, they know more about literacy from an early age than adults often realize. Evidence indicates that infants have awareness of print, and toddlers already grasp that letters mean things. Through various written and oral strategies, children express themselves and attempt to develop their abilities. For instance, when toddlers first learn to speak one-word sentences, they mean more than one word. In nursery school Mary was learning to talk. She would reach her arms up and say, "Up" meaning, "Please pick me up." At mealtime when Mary told, "More" the nursery teachers knew she wanted more food or drink. Although Mary was often unable to articulate more than one word, her one word represented many words. In the same way, children's early scribbling is an attempt to write. Children demonstrate a conscious effort to be literate through babbling and scribbling. To further their efforts, children require appropriate adult guidance and stimulating environments that encourage verbal and written communication and provide opportunities to explore. Language emerges, whether oral or written, comparably to children learning how to walk, when children have the necessity, opportunity, and proper guidance.

STAGES OF WRITING AND READING

Similar to other cognitive processes, writing goes through sequential stages. In the first stage, teachers observe that children pretend to write by scribbling horizontally. When scribbles become horizontal lines instead of aimless meandering, children show they understand that writing differs from drawing. This occurs usually at two years old. By three, children develop "pretend writing," a series of loops, tall sticks, and connected lines. Pretend writing is sometimes called "personal script" while teachers refer to mature writing as "conventional script." During this stage children often ask adults to read their pretend writing. If this occurs, teachers say, "Your writing looks so real. Can you tell me what it says?" In this way, children ascertain teachers support their efforts. After children tell what they wrote, teachers may write with conventional script beneath the children's pretend script. When talking to children about their pretend writing avoid terms like "wrong" or "nothing but scribbles." Instead teachers encourage children to use pretend write in various ways to excite them towards writing. They allow young children to "pretend write" on charts, make group stories, and label their artwork. Additionally, educators set up writing corners with ample paper and tools such as pencils, markers, rulers, templates, and scissors for children to practice and experiment on their own. A writing corner allows children to play with writing. Some writing corners' use items from offices to stimulate children to play they are office workers. Teachers' view any effort to write, whether pretend or conventional, as valuable.

Between three to five years of age, the next stage of literacy emerges where children begin to write alphabet letters. At this stage, teachers may combine traditional methods of copying with ideas that emphasize the meaning of writing like those above. Children begin to enjoy practicing their names, as the letters in their names have become clearer and excite them. They quickly learn the letters that belong to their names, ahead of most other letters. Their first efforts to print their name usually show letters of different sizes, sometimes upside down, and scattered. Teachers provide children with fun opportunities to explore writing their name and to enhance the meaning of writing such as signing holiday cards and labeling their things. Gradually, children print their names more evenly in linear manner. Regarding other letters than those in their name, children first distinguish whether a letter looks straight or curved. They pick up rounded letters first, and then curved lines. Slowly they learn letters with diagonal lines such as K and X.

Whatever methods educators use to further children's writing they remember to make it fun for children and ensure that children learn it meaningfully. The technique of learning must not supersede the main point that writing is communicating ideas. Too much stress on copying, without putting it in a meaningful context, makes accuracy in copying letters more important than writing for communication. Helping to make writing authentic, teachers encourage children to copy letters in a multitude of ways such as creating books, making signs, writing letters to their parents, and thank you cards.

Similar to activities that helps children learn the value of writing, reading activities should convey the importance of communicating ideas. Some methods teaching children to read over involve children in decoding schemes without understanding its association to communication. For instance, the phonics method can solely focus on letter sounds as a parrot game and assume children will derive meaning later. Too much sounding out leads children to believe reading involves making the correct oral response for the word they see. These types of lessons have to accompany other activities that keep reading in a contextual frame where meaning remains paramount. Teachers can ask children to draw pictures to accompany the words they read or they can have children read phrases or words in an enjoyable story. Especially, the love of stories and discussing them must accompany any efforts to read.

Reading, like writing and other cognitive areas, occurs in universal stages. When children first read a letter, generally they see every letter as a new, unrelated letter. Each letter 'A' is new and unrelated to any other 'A'. They do not understand that letters stay the same regardless of their context and size. Initially when children scan letters, they do not scan from left to right; rather they scan from many directions. Children may say the letters by rote such as singing the alphabet song, but do not see relationships. Usually between the ages of three to six, after being introduced to letters in many ways, they recognize letters stay the same despite varying contexts. Eventually, children begin to attach sounds to the letters and visa versa. Later they recognize that a series of letter combinations can be transformed into words.

Learning occurs best when it is fun, meaningful, sensorial, and not in isolation. When teachers integrate literacy events within other activities, using every opportunity available, they appreciate better the importance of literacy. For instance, during cooking class teachers include a written recipe. At holiday times children make a card for home and sign it. When a story excites them, teaches have the children springboard off of it and make their own books. Teachers employ a variety of activities that allow children to play and teachers to model. In this way, children demonstrate to themselves the value of reading and writing.

OBTAINING SPEECH

Children rapidly go from being nonverbal to language acquisition. Although several theories by psycholinguists attempt to describe this phenomenon, it remains a mystery. One exciting theory by Lev Vygotsky explains that infants learn through external speech derived from the dialogues between adults and infants. Infants pay careful attention when their caretakers' speak to them and develop their own whispered or silent monologues that Vygotsky called "inner speech." Inner speech, he theorized, emerges before oral skills and makes children capable of real thought. When children explore and talk to themselves they evolve language and other concepts.[45]

Parallel to Vygotsky, Sarkar theorized regarding language. However, his theory offers new profound concepts that educators will carefully have to think through such as the involvement of Cosmic or Universal Mind in language acquisition:

> "In that fluidal flow of cognition, bubbles are created. These bubbles are the bubbles of ideas…These ideas are the reflections or refractions of Cosmic Ideas. When these ideas concern the unit, the unit "I" tries to express them through his own psycho-physical structure. It endeavors to express its unit desires and longings according to the vocal chord and its hormone secretions. These reflections or refractions of ideas are expressed either within

or without. The expression within is called "inner voice" and the expression without is called "outer voice". The expressions within and without are collectively called language...So far as the refraction of the bubbles is concerned, the language of the universe is the same, was the same, and will remain the same forever. The language of the "inner voice" is always one and indivisible. Only in the outer manifestation do we get so many languages."[46]

Although educators still ponder over language acquisition, they do already know that the drive to communicate lies inherent in all humans. Unless prevented or thwarted, children work hard to accomplish speech. Generally, if children do not have good language acquisition during the early critical years, their lack effects their thinking and learning abilities for the rest of their life.

Educators know that if children come from a verbally rich environment that challenges the children to communicate often, most children will speak early and well. Successful language development requires two factors. First, a stress-free environment that promotes open communication so children communicate in a supportive atmosphere. Secondly, children have to feel motivated to learn; their relationships and environment ought to encourage them to ask questions, wonder, and express emotions. When children have eager listeners, they learn that language is an important tool at their command.

LEARNING IS NATURAL

What does the teacher know about language and literacy? As writer John Muir aptly said, "When we try to pick out anything by itself, we find it hitched to everything else in the universe."[47] Everything correlates. Speaking, writing, reading, reasoning, and playing relate. When teachers provide children with a happy, open, and supportive atmosphere, they enjoy learning. Where children have good role models and frequent opportunities to communicate, the children learn to express their ideas well. In a fun, print-rich environment with good personal guidance, reading becomes as essential as walking, writing as ingrained as holding a spoon.

I BELIEVE I CAN FLY

Close your eyes and see a red flower. Notice how dark its red petals appear.
Smell the sweet fragrance it offers and touch its soft, velvety petals.
Let the flower get bigger and bigger until you can sit on its petals.
When it is very large, you hear the flower's song. Hear the flower whisper to you.

Cognitive exploration happens when children discover the world as it is, while fantasy and creativity entail children seeking the world in ways it is not. Although both are natural and important, Neo-humanist educators recognize fantasy and creativity as characteristic of higher functions belonging to the deeper unconscious mind. They observe young children regularly and spontaneously journey between the unconscious and conscious layers. Whereas access to these deeper reservoirs in adults, comes only occasionally. By fostering children's creativity and imagination throughout childhood, Neo-humanist educators hope children will maintain a greater array of expressive, creative abilities when they mature.

FANTASY

Fantasy allows the mind to see things in uncommon ways. Unbridled and unrestrained imagination is a jumping board to creativity or original expression. Children have a natural drive to play with the world in unusual ways. Fantasy play provides opportunities for children to know the world in curious ways and to explore their inner selves more deeply. Accepting fantasy means taking risks as it leads to new experiences and relationships. In the past, psychodynamic theorists realized the value of fantasy as indicators of the unconscious mind. They utilized fantasy primarily for therapeutic purposes. Neo-humanist educators credit fantasy with more significance. Fantasy prevails as a major current in the flow of learning. Neo-humanist teachers wish for children to keep their bridge to higher cognitive functions, so they employ fantasy regularly in education. As Sarkar emphasized, "The child's mind is filled with fanciful imagery, and so the literatures (and teachers) will also have to soar in the sky of imagination with outstretched wings."[48]

To further a child's fantastical journey, teachers encourage it in children's play in various ways. Lying in the grass and naming cloud shapes is a common imaginative game. Ad-libbing stories about the various cloud shapes children see takes the game a step further. "I see a horse in the sky. There are many other animals with the horse. They are going to see the king." Using their imagination, teachers can invent various nonsensical games. For example, Jamie, a teacher of four-year-olds introduced a stimulating and fun game. She begins, "I have three eyes and ten noses." Joining in the game a child retorts, "I have two mouths and four ears." "Well I have four arms and purple hands" she replies. "My hair is green and blue and I have the biggest nose" tells another. This creative batter goes on and grows sillier, thrilling the children.

Educators also stimulate fantasy in children through visualizations. Creating vivid visualizations around metaphors for various themes animates higher thought in children. For instance, Lee, a teacher of five-year-olds, asked her children to close their eyes and imagine they were walking down a road with green grass on either side of it. Ahead down the road, they saw their home. Walking faster they soon reached the front door of their house. They opened the door and walked in. Slowly they looked around at the first room, noticing the tables and chairs. In one corner, they saw a table with a vase of flowers. Walking across the room, they went closer to the flowers. They saw its beautiful colors and smelled its sweet fragrance. At this point Lee asked her children to open their eyes and tell her about the flowers they saw.

"Children also naturally like fantasies and stories . . . Love of play and stories are liked equally by a child, and so should be utilized to the fullest advantage,"[49] remarked Sarkar. Fantastical stories catch the children's interest. Stories in which the characters converse with fairies, save a baby deer, and fly on a magic carpet. Of the many fantastical stories, children especially enjoy fairy tales. Some educators wonder whether traditional fairy tales overly scare children such as when the witch is pushed into an oven in *Hansel and Gretel*. Generally, though, teachers find that children adjust to fairy tales by engendering them with their own personal meaning. The witch in that story may represent an angry mother and killing the witch symbolizes extinguishing her anger. In this way fairy tales give creative outlets, and they also provide for therapeutic openings.

Besides fairy tales, drama is one of the best ways for children to experience fantasy and creativity. Young children begin dramatization by pantomiming and acting out events of familiar characters such as mothers, doctors, and dogs in their play. As children progress and gain dramatic skills, teachers branch off to a variety of theatrical experiences, a favorite being the dramatization of well-known stories such as *The Three Bears*. In this type of dramatic play children enjoy choosing their character roles. When children frequently dramatize, they investigate different types of roles and eventually even shy children will explore outgoing characters. Children's first effort to dramatize stories requires considerable coaching from the teacher, but gradually children's abilities expand. As they gain confidence, teachers discover children will divert from the original story with new ideas.

Similar to other areas, dramatic play goes through various stages of development. Teachers familiar with the universal stages of dramatic play enjoy witnessing the process, as it is similar to watching a caterpillar turn into a butterfly. Children "pretend play" first by acting out familiar routines. Initially they need to use some props to pretend. For instance, a spoon invokes the drama of cooking or a stick conjures a marching band. As they progress in their fantasy, children do not need to use many props. If they do, they tend to use elaborate props. They will find many items to make a detailed fantasy environment. At this level of dramatic play they assign or accept roles and may suddenly switch roles without warning. Children from four to six years old increasingly use language to create and enrich the plot, and they begin to make exciting and dangerous themes such as playing super heroes. As they mature, the characteristics of their roles develop, and they create a wider range of themes, ideas, and details.

MUSIC

Of all the arts, music holds one of the most favorite and universal forms. It inspires many different moods and emotions and opens the heart and unleashes creativity. Music exists in silence, in the noise of children's play, and in the flow of masterpieces. Possibly, music bridges the mundane to the super-mundane realm more than anything else, flowing easily from every day joys and sorrows to transcendental reverence.

Music frolics in nature and inside each person, therefore teachers arrange for children to experiment with tapping coconut shells, homespun maracas, various drums, and other instruments. Simple experiments such as playing scales on water glasses delight children's creativity. Instructors can place wind chimes in the playground, bells on the doors, and allow music to surround children. Through a musical environment, children can intuit more about themselves, their moods, and deeper stirrings. Playing a variety of music that invokes different emotions assists children in their exploration of themselves. As Elizabeth Barret Browning wrote,

"With stammering lips and insufficient sounds, / I strive and struggle to deliver right / The music of my nature."[50]

When music becomes an integral part of the early childhood curriculum, it not only develops musical abilities and appreciation, but it also enhances other aspects of development. Children respond with great enthusiasm to music. In a school setting, teachers apply music in various ways, guiding children in music appreciation, experimenting with instruments, and combining music with other activities. Especially effective is when teachers set aside daily singing times. Daily songs develop the children's oral language and musical enjoyment, ranging in spirit from fun to sacredness. In a friendly and relaxed atmosphere, music time becomes a special time where teachers and children share and develop closer social bonds.

While encouraging children to explore their own musical creativity, expose children to others' gifts through music. Children enjoy classical music if they are introduced to it properly, and classical music makes for calm and stimulating background music. When acquainting children with the classics, choose pieces such as the "Flight of the Bumblebee" and the "Carnival of Animals" that excite their imagination. When possible, let children attend children's dramas and concerts, for it is never too soon to introduce children to the classics. The depths in classical musical reaches out to the young children and will stir them.

VISUAL ART

Sarkar considered visual art an exceptional medium, as artists transform sculptures and pictures into pieces that seem alive and passionate. Beautiful art captures us with its vivid and moving qualities, bringing depth and excitement in the curvatures of clay or onto a canvas. Learning to draw, similar to other cognitive areas, passes through universal stages. Generally children younger than two years old make random marks with color when they learn to draw. From two to three years old, they begin to scribble. Sometime between the ages of two and four, the scribbles take on the outline of shapes such as circles, squares, and triangles. Between three and five years old, children make designs out of shapes, usually starting with drawings that look like suns (circle with rays) and mandalas (circle with a cross inside it). Then between the ages of four and five, their designs take the form of humans (circle with two appendages). Children draw many figures by time they are five years old such as animals, trees, and people. Wise teachers do not mistake and minimize early art by thinking of it as just scribbles. Instead scribbles occupy a natural stage through which children must pass. Recognizing each stage enables teachers to watch the remarkable development of their children's art.

CREATIVITY

Creativity is original expression, regardless of the form, whether found in visual art, drama, music, or movement. Creativity is the stepping aside from others' influences, expressing something just of oneself or something new for the first time. Naturally, as everyone grows older and undergoes a layering of influences, creative freshness becomes rarer. Children, as they have fewer impressions of the world, express creativity more often. They look at the world from their own original perspective with the same initiative as artists, musicians, and scientists. As Pablo Picasso said, "Every child is an artist. The problem is how to remain an artist once he grows up."[51]

To enhance children's creativity teachers remember that creativity is a process not a product. Exploration gives rise to and perpetuates creativity. Unfortunately some teachers put stress on the finished product rather than the creative process. Young children lose interest when the emphasis is on the finished product. When children receive varied opportunities to explore, whether with art materials, musical instruments, or dramatic movement, their creativity is nourished. Adults must not forget that creative noise and messiness go hand in hand with young children. Out of explorative mayhem comes children's works of art. Young children want to be at liberty to spontaneously manipulate, experiment, and pretend.

Despite children's natural enthusiasm and originality, they loose creativity in the wrong educational system. In such systems children learn experimenting gets them into trouble. Teachers inhibit students' creativity in the classroom in all too familiar ways such as directing every student to do the same art project and teaching there is only one right way to do it. Instead of allowing choices and an array of explorative opportunities, rigid teachers provide mediocre and uncreative activities. Sterile teaching creates an atmosphere that emphasizes time limits and singles out the "best" students. Worst of all, substandard teachers never use the word fun. When children cannot express themselves uniquely and freely, their creativity and imagination may fade. There is a story by an unknown author about the effect two teachers had on a child's creativity called, "My Purple Teepee".

> In first grade, Mr. Lohr said my purple teepee was not realistic enough, that purple was no color for a tent. He told me it was the color for people who died. Consequently, my drawing wasn't good enough to hand in with the others.
>
> I walked back to my seat counting the swish swishes of my baggy corduroy trousers. With a black crayon, nightfall came to my purple teepee in the middle of an afternoon. It became my favorite crayon that year in school projects.
>
> In second grade, Mr. Barta said, "Draw anything. I don't care what you draw. Surprise me with whatever you want."
>
> I sat staring at my paper, white and blank. When Mr. Barta came to my desk, my heart beat like a tom-tom. With his big hand he touched my head gently and said in a soft voice, "The snowfall. How clean and white and beautiful."

Teachers advance children's creative efforts by arranging opportunities for children to explore and by their acceptance and encouragement. Successful comments to give children about their creative efforts are: "You worked a long time on your project." "You were very concentrated." They avoid disastrous criticisms that undermine children's creative process. When teachers use non-judgmental encouragement, children become freer to pursue their creative self. Whatever children do they want acceptance from adults but in a manner that places no value judgments on their work.

All creative endeavors — music, visual arts, drama, and fantasy allow children to explore their deeper selves. Inside each child lives a natural urge to create, regardless of the level of talent. By utilizing a variety of creative mediums, keeping in mind that the process enriches more than the finished product, educators provide children with hours of deep learning. Creative moments wait for children around every corner. "Inside you there's an artist you don't know about…Say yes quickly, if you know, if you've known it from before the beginning of the universe," tells Jalai ud-Din Rumi.[52]

IN THAT SPECIAL PLACE

> *"And the day came when the risk (it took) to remain tight in the bud*
> *Was more painful than the risk it took to blossom."*[53]
>
> *Anais Nin*

People waste much creative energy and time resisting change when they presume growth will likely prove painful. When teachers put into practice Neo-humanism, they realize "remaining tight in the bud" is more painful than blossoming. Granted, it takes effort to bring together all the pieces and express them through ones teaching and learning environment. But no other way wins a child's heart more than teachers pushing beyond their limits for the sake of their students and ultimately for their own sake.

LEARNING ENVIRONMENT

In many ways the learning atmosphere and environment becomes an end product of Neo-humanism. After understanding Neo-humanism's principles and concepts, its physical expression takes the form of the environment, interactions, and atmosphere. Designing and creating an ideal learning environment tests the teacher's success. Is the environment inspiring, safe, and healthy? How does the environment effect relationships among children, among adults, and children to adults? Is it a natural environment, reinforcing the love of plants and animals? Does the environment provide many and varied opportunities for cognitive learning and creative development? Most importantly, does the environment reflect Neo-humanistic concepts and objectives?

The principles of Neo-humanism should positively affect all considerations of the classroom environment. Neo-humanist classrooms convey a feeling of family, safety, warmth, and at the same time bring a sense of order, curiosity, and creativity. Lush plants, ample lighting, splashes of color, and chairs in special groupings make up simple ways to improve the classroom. When young children sit in-group formations, not isolated in rows, they grasp and form collaborative relationships. A circular seating arrangement also provides ample opportunity for giving mutual respect.

Neo-humanist environments touch the artist in each child. Keeping this in mind, teachers hang decorations that have an aesthetic or learning value such as pictures related to the learning theme or copies of classical artwork that will enhance the room's atmosphere. Mindfully teachers display children's artwork and learning projects, careful not to clutter a room with pictures. Clutter causes a room to lose its sense of order and aesthetic appeal. Over all, the effect of the classroom, if carefully done, will stimulate and captivate the children's sense of contribution, beauty, and order.

Young children learn through their environment, so their surroundings make up a key part of their learning experience. An effective display is as important as the exciting materials. Often too many materials in a crowded space only distract the children. Organizing the room into specific learning corners, improves the children's focus as children can clearly see the separate groupings of activities and identify what the teacher has in mind for them to learn in each area such as a block corner, art area, puzzle area, and book area. By dividing the room in this manner, exploration and curiosity are bolstered, and concentration is enhanced.

SAFETY

Safety is a weighty consideration, a major concern. Good safety practices are characteristic of good care and love for young children. Teachers must keep the environment psychologically and physically safe, thus enhancing their students growth. To a child, what is a safe environment? Children require an environment where they feel comfortable, secure, and respected. An atmosphere of humiliation and fear harms character and impedes learning. A feeling of security grows through warm and consistent adult interactions, and where pleasant talk and laughter fills the air. Young children want hugs and pats of reassurance. During morning greetings, moments of distress, and free times, teachers may hold and put children on their laps. Insecure young children, who find separating from their parents difficult, may require extra support. For instance, four years old Rani cried if she was not at her teacher's side throughout the day. In her first days, Rani clung so closely that she acted like her teacher's third leg. This passed after a few days because her teacher consistently demonstrated to Rani a willingness to be there for her and meet her needs. For all young children, friendly physical behavior allows them to quickly gain confidence and security.

Unlike older children, preschool children demand adult supervision at all times. They are curious and may play with dangerous things such as electric outlets or cords. Good teachers anticipate possible dangers and remove them. They have to set up and maintain a classroom environment that prevents injuries. From the onset, educators involve children in following common safety practices within every activity area such as no hitting with any toy. Teaching safety means to remind children to follow safety practices and to stop or redirect unsafe child behavior. When the environment feels safe and teachers value safety, gradually children learn to protect themselves and to look out for others.

HEALTH

Teaching health in Neo-humanism means creating a healthy environment, promoting good health habits, and encouraging vegetarianism. A teacher sets up an environment that maintains and promotes good health. Similar to safety, teachers model good health habits daily and schedule them in the classroom setting. They provide the essential ingredients for maintaining good health such as exercise and rest. Young children require a balance of exercise and rest. Teachers arrange adequate indoor and outdoors space for games that exercise children's large motor muscles. Songs and dance make up good activities to regularly provide children exercise, and such exercises tone the muscles, increase appetite, and make rest easier. Although young children seem to be always moving, they require quiet and restful moments as well. Rest time or regular quiet activities such as reading and story telling needs to be included in the day's schedule. A balance of active and calm activities promotes children's health.

VEGETARIANISM

Regarding diet, Neo-humanist schools advocate vegetarianism for many reasons. First, vegetarians eat the most nutritious food. An adequate variety of vegetables, grains, and legumes make strong and healthy people. Meat has proven to be less healthy and unnatural for human beings. Strokes, heart disease, cancer, kidney disease, arthritis, and diabetes are some of the major illnesses that correspond to meat eating diets. In addition to health, vegetarianism is politically important because meat-eating habits have direct links to world starvation. For example eighty to ninety percent of all grain grown in America feeds animals grown for slaughtering. A Harvard nutritionist, Jean Mayer, estimates that reducing meat production by just ten percent would release enough grain to feed sixty million people.[54]

Neo-humanism also professes love for all creation. Although life exists by living off other life forms, Neo-humanists encourage eating from the lower end of the food chain. Most animals live many years and a meat diet disrespects their wish to live a natural life cycle. On the other hand, people harvest plants near the end of the plants' life cycle, thus eating vegetables and fruits gives a more harmonious diet. By offering vegetarian food, children learn to respect and consider the right of animals more, a vital aspect of Neo-humanism.

COMING TOGETHER

All components in creating the environment such as the physical arrangements, safety, and health come together to exclaim good learning, well being, and Neo-humanism. All the pieces come together to build a whole greater than the sum of its parts. In Neo-humanist schools, the classrooms sing the song of union, wonder, hope, and joy. Neo-humanism and the classroom environment it inspires provide for the well being of people. T.H. Robsjohn-Gibbings wrote, "Why do we love certain houses, and why do they seem to love us? It is the warmth of our individual hearts reflected in our surroundings." [55]

PUTTING IT ALL TOGETHER

> *"Train yourself in the ideal of the lily that blossoms in the mud and has to keep itself engaged*
> *In the struggle for existence day in and day out, parrying, bracing, and fighting*
> *The shocks of muddy water and storms and squalls and sundry and other vicissitudes of fortune;*
> *And yet it does not forget the moon above. It keeps its love for the moon constantly alive."*[56]
>
> Sarkar

Neo-humanism consists of a love affair with the moon, which here represents loving Infinite Consciousness. The philosophy came from Sarkar's vision of how to maintain humanity's most precious aspect, love. Neo-humanist teachers love their work with children and are inspired by the profound depths that their work can reach.

Although Neo-humanism took birth in 1982, Sarkar understood that when labor is truly noble it involves a timeless effort that has seeds in the hoary past and exists in the dawn of future glories. By enriching age-old ideas with the universality, dynamism, and equality of Neo-humanism, education moves towards the perennial source of inspiration. Educators cannot accomplish this movement by words and wishes; rather it involves a tireless effort to improve oneself and the entire educational process. Neo-humanist education certainly belongs neither to the weak-minded nor negligent. Unfortunately, great tasks appear daunting, and generally people are reluctant to undertake them. As Sarkar aptly put:

"Today's humanity is in despair; people think too much about their imperfections. They think, "Can I do it?" But in that supreme, Neo-humanistic status, they will say, "Yes, I am a Neo-humanistic being and I am destined to do great work – for that I have come on this earth. So there is no scope for doubt whether I can do it or not."[57]

Neo-humanist teachers reassure others beginning their educational process that it makes for a fascinating journey with many rewards. Sarkar told, "If, even then, someone says, "No, darkness is good for me!" – we will tell them, "All right, darkness is good for you, but just once why don't you come and see the light – it is even better!"[58]

Being a Neo-humanist educator means one can tap a perennial source of inspiration, which fills teachers when they become empty and enhances their labor. As their effort to love has no bounds, and includes the community, animals, and things, their inspiration has no end either. By grasping the universal picture and the uplifting concepts, they feel less alone and appreciate their work in new ways. Their daily relationships and toil become transformed into a work of art, a spiritual endeavor. As in the common saying, "Beauty lies in the details," with Neo-humanism, each day has splendid moments and challenges. Neo-humanistic teachers deeply appreciate the enormous impressions they make on their young, sensitive students and hold school life to be precious. They water, weed, and care for the blossoming children in the garden of school life. They share a wealth of wonders and the little children offer many flowers. Sarkar beautifully summed up the spirit of Neo-humanist education in the following anagram:

E - Enlargement of mind
D - DESMEP (Discipline, Etiquette, Smartness, Morality, English -lingua franca of the world, Pronunciation)
U - Universal outlook

C - Character
A - Active habits
T - Trustworthiness
I - Ideation of the Great
O - Omniscient Grace
N - Nice Temperament[59]

YOGA IN SCHOOLS

BY MJ GLASSMAN

Neo-humanistic education is deeply entwined with the ancient practice of Yoga. The practice of Astaunga Yoga in school acts as a cornerstone for student's spiritual, physical and social development. It is the foremost method for children to gain greater self awareness. Because of its importance this chapter will be entirely devoted to it.

WHAT IS YOGA?

While there are 8 major domains or branches that define yoga, most people think of the physical postures or asanas when we speak of yoga. Yet more and more interest in the fullness of yoga is finding its way into the mainstream of educators who are looking for a more comprehensive and meaningful curricula. The 8 limbs of Astaunga Yoga include:

1. Yama ~ The 5 keys guide spiritual aspirants in their external relationships with others and the world.
2. Niyama ~ The 5 keys that guide spiritual aspirants in understanding and balancing their internal thoughts and feelings.
3. Asana ~ Therapeutic body postures that are comfortably held.
4. Pranayama ~ Breath awareness and balance.
5. Pratyahara ~ Sense withdrawal from the external world.
6. Dharana ~ Mental focus and meditation.
7. Dhyana ~ Sustained concentration on the Divine.
8. Samadhi ~ The fullest expression of being human is realization of one's Oneness with the Cosmos.

Astaunga yoga is a systematized process for the progressive evolution of the body-mind-spirit. All Astaunga yoga practices guide children towards the goal of becoming an ideal human being. These yoga experiences contribute to maximizing their potential, guiding them to the fullness of all that they can be. All activities are adapted for young children so that they are age appropriate.

Children are encouraged to consider themselves as being more than a physical body. They are spiritual beings who guard and nurture the Inner Radiance in themselves and in others. What is a "yoga experience" for children? Yoga is any interaction, activity, or experience that involves any of the 8 domains of astaunga yoga--not just asana postures—which have been adapted to the interests of children.

DEVELOPMENTAL AWARENESS

Young children between the ages of 3-5 years of age are entering a highly creative and intuitive developmental phase and so it is essential that the yoga experiences reflect these aspects. The young child's primary quest concerns: 1) Attachment (Who loves them), 2) Identity (Who they are), and 3) Competency: (What they can do). The practice of yoga is where all three of these sectors intersect.

SECTOR 1: ATTACHMENT – WHO LOVES THEM.

In interactions with students the facilitator always has opportunities when she is physically affectionate and caring with the students. She can give a touch on the head or shoulder, a tap on the back, a playful wiggling of the foot as well as verbally caring such as "I love your snake pose." "That is an excellent choice." "I love how gentle you are with your friends." "you are such a good friend."

The facilitator is always looking for ways to let children know that they are loved by the teacher, loved by the other children, and, whenever appropriate, loved by the Divine. How can we refer to the Divine in a universal way and in a way that respects the diversity of the various religious paths that may be represented by the families in a classroom? This, of course, varies from community to community and requires some thoughtfulness. Yoga is theistic so it is important to find some acceptable way in which the class can refer to the Creator. Universal terms can sometimes be effective: "Inner Light," "Mother Earth," "The Force," "Mother Nature," or concepts that reflect in a universal manner something much greater than one's self.

SECTOR 2: IDENTITY – WHO THEY ARE

By bringing into the class affirmations and framing all interactions with positivity, the teacher can support children in being all that they can be. Children can be the Helpers of the Universe. They are the Light of the World. To help children embody this concept, facilitators invite children to stand with their feet wide on the floor, stretching their arms high, and they say, "Shine your Heart Lights into the world. Shine happiness on the trees. Shine happiness on the animals and on your mommies. Shine your Heart Lights on _____ (a sad classmate.)"

Young children are searching for their place in the world. Like the coach inspiring the sports team to be enthusiastic, to do great things, to be all that they can be ~ the facilitator brings words of inspiration, words of happiness, words for overcoming fear and self doubt into the asana class. Children may hold a standing lunge position with arms stretched upward (Warrior Pose) and repeat loudly "I am a super star! I am awesome!" Encouraging children to repeat these words loudly has the power to root these qualities in their hearts and to believe in their Divine Potential.

SECTOR 3: WHAT THEY CAN DO - COMPETENCY

No doubt they can hop like rabbits, slither like snakes, fly like the bats, roar like lions, sway like the elephants. Just as the early yogis learnt from and named asanas (postures) after the diversity of beings that populate the world, facilitators encourage physical motions with the characteristics of these animals. Be brave like the tiger. Be strong like the bear. Be graceful like the flamingo. Be fearless like the giraffe. Be swift to get away from a bad situation like the crow. Be gentle like the feather. Be sweet like the honey bee. Be beautiful like the flower. Be loud like tyrannosaurus Rex. Be quiet like the turtle. Be helpful like the dog. Be loving like the cat.

Competency in Yoga also includes enabling young children to see and understand how their actions effect others, essentially the laws of cause and effect. What happens when you use a loud voice, gently pat someone on the back, hit someone, tell someone "I like your smile," or say "Can I play with you?" Facilitators constantly are coaching children as to why certain behaviors and actions are preferable and why some are undesirable. They can call positive actions, "warm fuzzy," and undesirable behavior, "cold and prickly." Empathy and kindness are constantly reinforced and discussed at every opportunity.

YOGA DOMAINS 1 & 2: YAMA AND NIYAMA

Yama and Niyama comprise the ethical foundation of yoga and are the first domains of Yoga. They are ancient guidelines for cooperative living and compassionate lifestyle. Here is a simplification for 3-5 year old children:

Ahimsa: Kindness, No hurting. *I am friendly. I wear my "warm fuzzies" every day.*
Satya: Honesty. Consideration. *I speak up for myself and others.*
Asteya: Responsibility. No grabbing. *I take responsibility for my actions.*
Brahmacharya: Mutual respect. Unconditional love. *We are different and I love you.*
Aparigraha: Simple living. *Just two will do.*
Shaocha: Cleanliness. Orderliness. *I put away what I use.*
Santosha: Contentment. Acceptance. *I am happy. I can "move on".*
Tapah: Self-restraint. Patience. *I like to help and take care of my friends.*

Svadyaya: Understanding. *I like to learn what my friends like.*
Iishvara Pranidhana: Spiritual focus. *I take shelter in "Goodness".*

YAMA AND NIYAMA IN THE CLASSROOM

Yama and Niyama concepts are introduced in the classroom through conversation, songs, discussion, stories, artistic expression, and dramatic play, including puppets. There are many benefits from them. By providing a clearly defined moral foundation for interaction, it reduces stress, frustration, and confusion. The guidelines support the children in properly caring for themselves and others. They enhance a sense of safety and comfort, and establish harmony in the classroom. The classroom's ethics create a small microcosm of what the world can be like. Lastly, ethics enable the young child to catch a glimpse of the Infinite in everything.

YOGA DOMAIN 3: ASANAS

The young child can be highly egocentric and is becoming increasingly aware of the complexities of relationships. As they begin to form relationships with the world, they tend to ascribe personal thoughts and feelings to all living beings: rocks, trees, and animals. Eager to embrace the magical aspects of life, yoga experiences are a wonderful venue for deepening their yearning to understand the mechanics of the world around them, as they explore everything, trying to make sense out of the adventure of life.

So yoga experiences for young children are expressed in the way they learn best ~ through exploration, experimentation, imitation, and creativity. Imaginative play is their bridge to reality and their methodology for learning and understanding, internalizing from experience and exploration rather than through instruction and direction.

Asanas are postures comfortably held and presented in a way that includes movement, breath awareness, sensory involvement, focus, creativity, and fun. It is important that these adventures be in alignment with developmentally age appropriate best practices. Still discovering what their bodies can do, they thrive on investigating the world through their motor organs: jumping, hopping, spinning, crawling, rolling, flying, as well such as catching, throwing, pushing, and pulling. Arms, hands, legs, knees, and feet are engaged in active and relaxing movements. The sensory aspect is of special importance. This means showing visual pictures, making sounds, and providing kinesthetic experiences (poses that engage the hands, feet, and skin) whenever possible.

While many poses may initially resemble adult postures, they quickly morph into the world of fantasy, play, sound, and movement since this is how the young brain is wired for learning, understanding, and integrating within their being.

How is yoga asana introduced to young children?

When interacting with very young children, it is important to fully understand the developmental and brain needs of each child. As you can imagine, asana experiences for the young child are substantively different than what one would see in an adult asana class. The young child loves repetition and will enjoy repeating their yoga experiences over and over. Engagement of all the senses is paramount along with increased doses of creative movement, sound, and imagination. Every pose is enlivened and energized.

ASANA METHODOLOGY

At the base of asana learning is repetition. Repeating poses supports the development of determination and perseverance. Young children love repetition! The poses make physiological changes to the children. Crawling on hands and knees and crossing the front mid-line of the body engages both hemispheres of the brain. Placing the tongue on the roof of the mouth is calming. This can be done in Balance poses. Young children's bones and muscles are not fully formed so poses such as shoulder stand and other poses may not be done well but can still be adapted.

Make sure that the yoga experience is going to appeal to boys and girls. Please review this list of possible asana choices and consider will some of these appeal to one gender more than another? Flower, princess, butterfly, fairy, ladybug, bird, bear, elephant, hammer, helicopter, warrior, train. In order to maintain a fun atmosphere and the active participation of all children, poses must reflect their gender and individual interests. Yoga games, stories, songs, art, drama, and other expressions of creativity may also be incorporated. Creative exploration activates many centers of the brain. When introducing a pose invite the children to find other ways to do it. Classes may be a wonderful mixture of teacher direction and student direction. Let playfulness prevail.

CLASS THEMES

Often children are exploring various themes in school. Nature and science concepts easily blend into the yoga experience such as: Reenacting a day in the life of a bear with its bearlike interations with friends, enemies, food, what it loves, what it avoids, and what it offers the earth community.

Dramatizing rain and their nurturing relationship with animals and plants.

The Clash and cohesion in the lives of mountain goats (Billy Goats Gruff).

The specialties of preying mantis, scorpion, ladybird, ant, and other insects.

When learning the same loving approach is shared with creatures which children may fear as the ones they like. These wondrous relationships are explored as children discover the diverse creatures and astonishing environments of our amazing planet, their value, and the gifts that they bring.

ASANA FLOW

The length of a yoga class will depend on how much time is available. It may range from 12 minutes to 30 minutes. Ideally the facilitator will develop a flow so the children can predict how the experience will unfold. Starting with a song, rhyme, or chant is a delightful way to bring everyone together. Having yoga cards or other representations can be helpful in guiding the class and with transitions between poses.

Yoga class has much experimentation. Often when children are given permission to self-express, they can become 'overly expressive' and excited. The facilitator will want to guide or redirect the flow from time to time. If the energy level is accelerating, what can she do to bring it down? Some background information about movement and energy can be useful. Here are some tips to assist the management of energy flow:

> Back bends and movement – Are energizing
> Forward folds and resting poses (stationary) – Are calming
> Twists – are neutral

So if the children have performed 2 or 3 asanas such as sharks, airplanes, and gorillas, the facilitator may want to choose calming poses like sleeping bears, rocks, snakes, and starfish-on the-ocean-floor to bring the energy level back down.

SOME EXAMPLES OF YOGA CLASS, FROM SIMPLE TO INVOLVED

The asana class may be as simple as having a few children select some asana cards and these poses are repeated for a time. The facilitator may point out interesting variations that other children are bringing to a pose. One pose can sometimes morph into others such as "Whot knows what sharks eat? What would they look like? Who are some other ocean friends? (Jellyfish, seaweek, sea turtle, etc.)" Blending asanas with other activities and books on the theme extends and compliments the learning.

Asana class can be more involved and integrated into a story and theme. Here is an example of "A Yoga Adventure to Africa."

We are going on Safari. We are walking in a circle, a circle a circle. Going to Africa (clapping hands), Africa, Africa.

It is far away (hand over eyebrow as if looking far away), far away, far away.

We are almost there (hand is moving from eyebrow to eyebrow as if wiping away sweat), almost there, almost there.

(Jumping up in air and then down). Here we are!

I see elephants walking!

Forward bend until hands and feet are on the ground. Everyone can walk forwards. 1,2,3,4,5,6,7,8 and then backwards, 1,2,3,4,5,6,7,8.

Let's interlace our fingers together and raise our trunks up high into the air.

Elephants can walk bent over swinging their trunks from side to side.

Elephants can eat leaves from the trees reaching high with their trunks. (Make smacking sounds with the mouth.)

Elephants can spray water on their friends. (Make shhhh sounds.)

Oh my goodness the elephants has accidentally stepped on the snake. (Scream).

Lay down on your tummies with foreheads on the ground. Legs are out straight behind the body. Hands are palms down on either side of the neck. "All snakes will wake up." Pressing down on the hands, everyone raises their chests and heads up, holding the pose (not the breath) for just a moment. Tongues may slither in and out of their mouths. Then all snakes hisssssss as they lower their bodes back to the ground. This can be repeated 4-5 times… as one elephant apologies over and over. (It was an accident. I'm so sorry…etc.)

The snake forgives the elephant since it was just an accident. The elephant didn't mean to hurt the snake. The elephant helps to lift the snake up into the acacia tree.

Everyone stands straight and tall in front of the wall or by a chair with their feet rooted in Mother Earth. Then they bend one knee and bring that foot to the inside of the base leg with the knee pointing out to the side. Palms come together over the heart and then are lifted up, up over the head. As the arm trunks straighten, the palms open, spreading apart, like a tree branch. Children may lean against wall behind them or place one hand on the chair.

Children can be individually invited to share who they see in Africa and can invent a movement or pose that matches their animal of choice. (Gorilla, lemur, hippo, zebra, wildebeest, piranha, crocodile, etc.) Each pose can be repeated 4-5 times.

Oh the sun is setting. It is time for everyone to find a place to sleep. Show me how monkeys sleep? They sleep high in the trees on a lovely branch so I want everyone to find your special branch and lie down. What sounds do you think they make?

Let's lie on our backs with our hands on our tummies. Feel as we breathe in, the tummies rise high like the mountain and as we breathe out (blowing breath), they come down. Breathe up. Breathe down. Breathe up. Breathe down. Watch your hands on your tummy go up and down. Up and down. Remember all the animal friends that we saw today: the big elephant, the skinny snake .... (continue with naming animals), and oh yes, the tree... which is where we made our beds today. The closing can be a deep relaxation pose and meditation.

OCCUPY THE MIND WITH POSITIVITY

Young children experience a lot of stressors in their lives and often have a difficult time measuring up to the expectations of themselves and others. They experience fear of separation, 'not being good enough', and anxiety. In yoga class young children love the magical power of affirmations. These are important tools to protect their minds from negative, defective thinking. Sprinkling an occasional affirmation can support the development of their inner courage and stronger self-esteem.

I am kind.
I am a good friend.
I take care of my friends.

I am strong (brave, powerful).

I can do it!

These can be blended with powerful poses, such as warrior and hero postures. Affirmations are generally constructed in the present tense as a condition or ability that is possessed right now! They may be strongly affirmed with loud voices! As you become more familiar with the students and their life experiences, other affirmation ideas will emerge.

WHAT ARE SOME BENEFITS OF YOGA ASANA?

Yoga postures for young children are easy and not strenuous. The facilitator engages students in the culture of physical fitness, mental/emotional fitness, fun and caring for friends. Yoga postures strive to achieve all-round harmony of mind and body. Asanas can strengthen muscles and bones, increase flexibility, balance, and body awareness. They maximize effects on blood and lymph circulation, support and strengthen lungs and respiration, balance hormonal secretions, stimulate bone development, and regulate digestive activity. In fact, yoga asanas maximize the balance of all the physical systems of the body.

Perhaps the most apparent benefits that clinical research have shown are the many profound effects yoga has on the nervous system: reducing anxiety, inviting calmness, redirecting emotions, minimizing hyperactive and aggressive tendencies (temporarily), and balancing emotional moods. Yoga class provides laughter, joy, and positivity. It strengthens participants relationships and withdraws their minds from undesirable thinking.

Depending upon how one facilitates yoga, it can also build student's confidence and determination, support their positive attitude, reinforce tolerance, acceptance, and respect of others. It can enhance creativity and intuitiveness. During yoga, opportunities arise for conflict resolution, turn taking, and sharing.

At the root of yoga there is the spiritual aspect. And so the yoga experience invites a deeper caring relationship to the earth, humanity, and all living beings. It increases a desire to interact with others in a kind and harmonious way. Yoga asanas gradually improve interest and ability to meditate, awareness that we are more than our thoughts and emotions, and a sense of inner peace and contentment. Yoga asanas embody an acknowledgment of a Greater Force that is directing the amazing Dance of Creation.

DOMAIN 4: PRANAYAMA: THE SCIENCE OF BREATH

Yogis believe that prana is the life force that flows in and out of our bodies and all living beings. We take it in when we inhale and release it when we exhale. Prana is everywhere. Pranayama is the science of yogic breathing and is the fourth limb of Yoga. It involves controlling the movement of prana or energy through the use of various techniques. Every technique has a particular goal such as heating, cooling, soothing, and energizing.

Pranayama, breath control, is the heart of most practices and is what distinguishes yoga from other physical practices. Breathing is a natural and primarily involuntary process. Respiration oxygenates organs, muscles, cells, and soothes the nervous system. Pranayama incorporates proper diaphragmatic breathing where the chest opens and the lungs expand. Abnormal breathing frequently occurs high in the chest. This can trigger the fight or flight hormonal response and can manifest as breathing at a fast, shallow pace. Shallow breathing tends to overstimulate the sympathetic nervous system and can cause other general health problems.

In pranayama, usually breath is through the nose. Incoming oxygen is better filtered and purified with nasal breathing than through mouth breathing. Pranayama activates the relaxation response which calms the nervous system and lowers respiration and heart rate. The breath naturally becomes slower, facilitating an even deeper relaxation response.

HOW IS PRANAYAMA INTRODUCED TO YOUNG CHILDREN?

The breath rhythm has three basic parts: exhalation, inhalation, and the pauses in between. Most forms of yoga retention of breath and other adult practices are not recommended for children because the nervous system and lungs are not fully developed until years later. With younger children the emphasis is on the inflowing or inhalation and the out flowing or exhalation. This can be further simplified by saying 'breathing in' and 'breathing out'.

Many young children who experience high stress have already begun to develop improper breathing patterns. Unhealthy breathing can be imprinted on children by their parents. Breathing patterns have a profound effect on emotional well-being. It is the teacher's aim to support young children in the flowing ways:

To be able to slow down and deepen their breathing
To enhance their awareness of the breath
To provide abdominal breathing experiences
To increase their understanding of how breath can be used to manage stressed

Medical studies have confirmed that there is a correlation between breath, thought, and many physiological responses. A harmonious mind is created and sustained by slow, deep, and regular respiration. Proper breathing holds the key to a balanced mental state.

Yogic breathing is closely connected to the abilities of memory and learning. We learn better when the breathing is calm. The calmer and steadier the breathing is, the stronger the power of mental receptivity. So children's learning capacity can be enhanced with a calm body and calm mind. The retentive power wanes tremendously during physical or mental restlessness and anxiety.

Oxygen purifies the blood and is good for the nerves. Full oxygenation of the blood and organs invigorates the body, inspires the mind, and gives a sense of well-being and contentment. By learning the art of pranayama, children become aware of how a calm mind is associated with deep breathing.

PRANAYAMA METHODOLOGY

Breathing is taking in oxygen found in the air. What is air? The existence of something invisible such as air can be demonstrated with young children in many ways:

Blowing up balloons and allowing them to deflate around the room.

Making paper fans and then having the children fan themselves. "Can you feel that? Can you feel it touching your face?"

Taking students outside on a windy day and letting them observe the effects of the wind.

Blowing feathers and catching them.

SUPINE BELLY BREATHING

Children can become more aware of abdominal breathing with the following steps:

1. Children lie on their backs and place a small stuffed animal or toy on the belly of each child.

2. Close your mouth and breathe through your nose. Watch your toy go up and down as you breathe. Now it is going up. Now it is going down. Now it is going up. Now it is going down.

3. Use your breath to move the toy. (Continue for 1-2 minutes or until someone gets restless.)

YOGA BREATH CENTERING FOR YOUNG CHILDREN

There are various games involving breath to help children slow and center on the breathing process:

Ahhh Breath - Take a deep inhale breath followed by an exhaled "ahhhh breath while folding forward. (Seated or standing)

Balloon Breath – Take a breath. Place your hands on your belly button. When you breathe, breathe all the way down to your hands. Feel your tummy expand like a balloon? And then the ballon gets smaller and flat. Breathe into your balloon...and then let it go. What color is your balloon? Make your balloon belly really big. This be practiced lying down with the hand on the belly or with a toy on the belly. (Seated, standing, lying down)

Bee Breath – While seated, pretend you are a bee. Breathe into your balloon belly. When you are ready to exhale, make a very high-pitched "hum" like a bee. Make it loud. Make it long. Place your hands over your ears and do it again. This is fun to do while flying around the room!

Big Bird Breath – Children are standing. On the inflowing breath the wingtips are lifted high above our heads. On the out-flowing breath dive/bend forward and touch the wingtips to the earth.

Brave Breath – Deep inhale. Deep exhale. Repeat 3-5 times slowly. Can sometimes be practiced with a partner or teacher as well as in a circle with everyone holding hands.

Chopping Wood Breath – Stand with the feet hip width apart or wider and join your hands together as if holding an ax. On the inhalation, raise the ax up high overhead. Stop for a moment. On the exhalation, swing the arms downward, holding the ax, with a "ha" sound. Knees may or may not bend as the ax descends. On the inhalation, swing the ax high overhead once again. (The ax can transform into a hammer if they do not understand what an ax is).

Dragon Breath – Take a deep inhalation. Then on the exhalation: ROOOAAAARRR.

Mother Earth Breathing – Breathe in. I feel happy. Breathe out. I feel happy. All of Mother Earth's children are breathing with us. Raccoon, Eagle, Rabbit, Bear, Whale, Ant, Tree. They are all breathing with us. (Seated or supine)

Rabbit Breath – In a kneeling position inhale through the nose in 3 quick breaths. (Sniff. Sniff. Sniff.) Exhale out through the nose in a long breath, fold downward and bring the forehead to the earth.

Shhh Breath – Take a deep inhalation. Place your pointer finger on your lips and exhale a long ssshhhhhhhhhh while making eye contact with everyone in the room.

Snake Breath – While seated, simply inhale through the nose, then on the exhalation make a hissing sound, slowly, slowly. (The exhalation should be longer than the inhalation).

Sunshine Breath – Inhale as you reach up for Father Sun. Grab some sun! Exhale as you bring the handfuls of sun into your heart. Hold that sunshine in your heart with your hands. (Add a song or chant if you like).

Smell the Flower and Blow out the Candle – Curl your fingers a little on one hand so that it resembles an open flower with the palm facing up. Hold the pointer finger up on the other hand, pointing towards the sky. Smell the flower with your nose in your flower hand then lean towards the other hand and blow out the candle.

PRANAYAMA FLOW

Pranayama or creative breathing exercises can be practiced at the beginning of yoga class as a centering practice, go in the middle, or at the end. Often breathing exercises lead into chanting and meditation. It is very helpful to create breathing cards. Breath Cards can be made with photos of the children or pictures of the animals or plants represented in the breath exercises mentioned above.

When facilitating a breathing experience, remember that the goal is to achieve a particular uplifting and fun mental/emotional state of balance. This state of mind is the response to a physiological exercise. Consequently, all breath experiences should be repeated 3-5 times in order to bring this result. If a total of 1-3 breath cards, for example, are chosen, that is a total of perhaps 15 breaths to recalibrate the physical body in an effort to evoke the desired mental/emotional response. In addition, you will notice that all of these exercises have one thing in common. They all lengthen the exhalation breath. This is another essential part of this process.

When facilitating simple pranayama experiences, it is important to always surround these activities with the higher feelings of love, goodness, happiness, and that sense of being surrounded by love, caring, and positivity. These feelings maximize the benefit of the exercises.

Of course, breath exercises are not employed only for yoga class and meditation time. Breathing exercises with the breath cards can be used any time a child (or facilitator) is frustrated, angry, or off center...or if the energy level of the entire class is escalating. The facilitator invites a child to practice a Breath Card with a friend, the whole class, or the teacher at other times of the day. Encourage children to invent other breaths.

SUMMARY OF THE BENEFITS OF YOGIC BREATHING

Through attention to the breath, children tap into the fullness of who they are. Greater understandings shine through with a new, fresher perspective. Yogic breathing exercises can help to improve stress management and help overcome fear. Deeper, fuller breathing clears out stale air and improves the quantity of oxygen filling the lungs. When breathing is most efficient, fresh oxygen is supplied, the lungs are strengthened, and there is also an improved emotional stability. Children feel self-confident, self aware, and equanimity of mind. Pranayama directly effects the total functioning capacity of the brain and the nervous system. It supports better integration between the physical, mental, and other layers of our being. A regular pranayama practice during school time increases receptivity and focus. It reduces blood pressure, improves overall oxygenation of organs and cells, calms emotions, and results in more positivity.

DOMAIN 5: PRATYAHARA OR SENSE WITHDRAWAL

Sense withdrawal provides greater calmness and self-awareness. Usually children are very sensory occupied. Children need help in learning to withdraw from their senses. In yoga there are various methods to introvert the senses. Young children primarily learn it with the practice of Shavanansa or deep relaxation pose. The key goal of Shavasana pose, deep relaxation pose, is to induce a state of relaxation and to withdraw from the external environment by closing the eyes, the mouth, and resting the hands and legs. It is generally practiced lying prone on the ground. It can be presented at the end of the asana practice and/or as meditation.

HOW IS PRATYAHARA OR SHAVASANA INTRODUCED TO CHILDREN?

In the Shavasana pose the children lie down on their backs with arms at their side. Shavasana is beginning meditation. It is relaxing with mental alertness. Very young children may need some support calming their energy down. What kinds of experiences can the teacher include to facilitate serenity? Calming music, dimming the lights, speaking slower, speaking quieter, ringing a tiny bell, and so forth aid the children's efforts.

The shavasana experience can take many forms. A facilitator can read or tell a short story while children are lying in shavasana. Another is the use of short visualizations and imagery. Students can be reminded to close their eyes and paint pictures in their heads. Visualization assists them maintain focus and concentration by activating several brain centers. For instance, ask the children to imagine that the clouds in the sky are filled with love and they are pouring love down on them. They are bathing their bodies with love from head to toe.

Simple affirmations may be used here to support the students in achieving a relaxed and sweet state of being: I am calm. I am relaxed. I am OK. The teacher may sing *Baba Nam Kevalam* (Love is all there is) softly over and over or play briefly soft music. Be sure to allow a very brief time for stillness and quiet. The facilitator can gauge when to stop it. Here are examples of Shavasana experiences.

SHAVASANA WITH AFFIRMATION AND WINDING DOWN MOVEMENT

Ahhhhhhh. I am calm. I am peaceful. I am happy.
Raise your foot and drop it to the ground.

Raise your other foot and drop it to the ground.
Raise your arm and drop it to the ground.
Stick your tongue out and say ahhhhh. Put it back in your mouth.
Raise all your arms and legs and drop all of them to the ground.
Open your eyes and blink them 3 times. Then close them.
Ahhhhhhh. I am calm. I am peaceful. I am happy.

SHAVASANA AND VISUALIZATION:

"You are sitting in the lap of Mother Nature surrounded by the light of love. The Love Light is filling you up. The light is covering your feet, your legs, your tummy, your chest, your shoulders, your arms, your hands, your neck, and your head. Your whole body is filled up with light. You are shining like the moon at night. You are sitting in the lap of your Divine Friend who is always with you.... and who will always be with you...."

SHAVASANA FLOW

During the shavasana practice, the teacher may review points, comments, and ideas that were shared throughout the class about kindness, sharing, and gentleness. The facilitator puts an enormous focus on love and positivity. Remember that the mind is more malleable when relaxed. She may ask the children to say inside their heads, "I am Great. I am Good. I am Love." "We are Love. We are Light."

Initially the shavasana experience may be 1-3 minutes. The teacher observes the children for restlessness as to when the practice should end. She reminds the children to breathe in, make the tummy big, and breath out, make the tummy small. Shavasana is another time to nurture their relationship with every child by gently touching the head of every child.

SOME BENEFITS OF PRATYAHARA OR SHAVASANA

Pratyahara or Shavasana clears the mind, reduces stress, supports an inner connection, and magnifies the feeling of connection with the Shining Light Within. It can increase concentration, attention, and intuition.

DOMAIN 6 – DHARANA OR CONCENTRATED MEDITATION FLOW

In young children, Dharana is equivalent to meditation preparation by chanting. Chanting is the rhythmic speaking or singing of words or sounds. Chanting a mantra, sacred text, name of God, or other words is a commonly used ancient practice. There are two basic types of chanting. "Japa" or "personal chanting" is where one chants alone. Chanting in a group is called "kiirtan." Kiirtan is usually accompanied by musical instruments, clapping, as well as other movements and gestures. Young children particularly enjoy kiirtan.

CHANTING WITH A MANTRA

Mantra is the transformation of breath into sound. This sound may be a single syllable or a group of words. Clinical studies indicate that rhythmic breathing and repetition redirect negative thinking and can bring a more positive mental focus. The actual word "mantra" means "that which liberates the mind" so using mantra has the capability of uplifting moods and minimizing negative thinking patterns. It is extremely effective in transforming and balancing the emotional well-being of young children. Rabbi Shefa Gold said about chanting, "Chant is a bridge between the inner life and the outer expression, between the solitary practice and the shared beauty of fellowship. When we chant we are using the whole body as the instrument with which to feel the meaning of the sacred phrase." (http://www.rabbishefagold.com/about/, accessed June 12, 2017)

Many mantras are derived from the Sanskrit language. The Sanskrit alphabet is based on the inner sounds emanating from within the body, specifically from the 50 glands clustered around the chakra. Advanced meditators attuned their minds to these inner sounds and each sound became one letter. There are 50 glands, 50 sounds, and subsequently 50 letters in the Sanskrit alphabet. So the Sanskrit language is the human body's eternal song. The careful combination of Sanskrit letters can vibrate these glands, creating a powerful elevating effect on the mind.

Mantra is a tool that young children can use to direct the mind towards positivity. By engaging in a mantra practice, children choose the thoughts that define who they are-what they want to feel and believe. Mantra and kiirtan can be key to withdrawing the young mind from distractions and negativity. Chanting or singing mantra is a salve that heals the wound of disrupted peace during stressful times.

CHANTING AND KIIRTAN METHODOLOGY

When singing kiirtan, the breath becomes slow and deep due to the lengthy exhalations. Consequently, many of the benefits of pranayama, the science of breath, are applicable to chanting as both of these practices have the shared benefit of relaxing the sympathetic nervous system. With a calmer mind, children make the best decisions. Mental equipoise influences also their feelings of peace and harmony. Children pick up on each others' better feelings and thoughts when they are projected during chanting. This is how the world becomes a better place. Like a spiritual aspirant said, "If one does kiirtan from the bottom of one's heart, with full ideation and love even the trees, birds, and animals will respond. They will be deeply influenced. Such is the power of kiirtan. It brings the devotee face to face with God."

CHANTING TECHNIQUES

With young children, chanting may be with words and/or sounds that have meaning or no meaning, simply because they like to play and explore everything, including sound. The following are a few fun chanting experiences that can be shared with children either as part of the meditation practice or during a literacy activity:

The vowels: Ahhhhhh. AAAA. EEEEEE. IIIIII. OOOOOO. UUUUU.

Consonants" MMMM. SSSS. Shhhhh

Om. (The Cosmic or psychic sound of all living beings working together.)

International words for "Peace" such as Shanti (India). Paz (Portuguese/Spanish. Amani (Swahili). Salam (Eritrea).

International words for "Hello" such as Shalom (Israel). Jambo (Swahili). Aloha (Hawaii, U.S.). Namaskar (India). Konichiwa (Japan).

Affirmational chanting, i.e., Love is above me. Love is below me. Love is all around.

Baba Nam Kevalam. (Love is all there is)

The universal mantra, Baba Nam Kevalam (Love is all there is), is a favorite chant of children. Young children think and feel the meaning when they repeat this mantra silently or aloud. Facilitators can combine the meaning with the actual singing of the mantra. For example, "Baba Nam Kevalam. Love is all there is." Singing the mantra prior to meditation or even during meditation prepares the body-mind for stillness. All of the children can sing it together and while they are meditating, the facilitator can continue singing it softly. The chanting melodies may range from a simple monotone to a few notes to a highly complex melody. Any tune can accompany the mantra. When singing together, children love moving their hands: clapping, holding hands, and clapping parner's hands. They enjoying waving their arms, sweeping them overhead, behind the back, and so forth. And don't forget those feet: stomping, marching, twirling, and jumping. Dance movements can also be added.

VOCALIZATION OF MANTRA

There are five levels of chanting vocalization: 1) singing loudly, 2) softly, 3) a whisper, 4) only the lips moving (no sound), 5) inside (completely internal). Let the children experiment with the five levels.

POSITION

Chanting can be practiced with young children while sitting or standing, prior to meditation, during meditation, or during shavasana (yoga deep relaxation pose). A drum may be played, a bell chimed, a singing bowl engaged, or other instrumentation if desired to close the meditation.

CHANTING FLOW

Singing need not occur only during meditation. One may break out into a chant at any moment during the day. It is particularly effective when a child (or teacher) is experiencing sadness, frustration, or burnout in order to change a personal flow or the group flow. Chanting can also be expressed when feeling happy or joyful, or for absolutely no reason at all!

BENEFITS OF CHANTING

Chants, songs, and mantras provide "technical support" for young children in directing the mind toward a specific positive goal. Through this practice we are choosing the positive power that certain syllables evoke. Kabir said, "If you want the truth, I'll tell you the truth. Listen to the secret sound which is inside you. The One no one talks of…He speaks the secret to Himself and He is the One who has made it all." (Kabir, translated by Robert Bly (in "The Simple Purification," from *News of the Universe: Poems of Twofold Consciousness.* By Robert Bly, Counterpoint Press, 2015).

Chanting, Baba Nam Kevalam, is a method for regaining and maintaining peace during stressful times. When a child feels stressed, 5-10 minutes of focused chanting (especially external) can clear away negative thoughts that obstruct connection to Inner Harmony. Scientific studies indicate that repetition of certain sounds has a calming effect. When sad or frustrated, it can uplift the emotions and refocus the attention towards positivity. Singing Baba Nam Kevalam, as it is a mantra of love and connection, accelerates the speed of one's momentum towards achieving that

Supreme State of Balanced Being within. The mental clarity that comes from chanting, can help young children to find solutions to problems and can provide relief from physical and psychic ailments.

DOMAIN 7: DHYANA MEDITATION OR SUSTAINED MEDITATION

Meditation is the touchstone for self-transformation and ongoing spiritual development. It is the practice of quieting the body and filling the mind with the highest positive Good and holding it there for a while.

HOW IS SUSTAINED MEDITATION INTRODUCED TO YOUNG CHILDREN?

Since young children may find it difficult to focus on an idea or a point, often the "point" of focus is on sound. Yogic meditation is not emptying the mind of thoughts and maintaining a thought-free mental void. Yogic meditation is a process of guiding the thoughts and filling the mind with the Highest Good. This may be achieved in a variety of ways, but some time dedicated to mantra, the highest, subtlest of sounds, is essential. Baba Nam Kevalam, Love is Everywhere, is a favorite.

It takes time and practice to focus the thoughts. The young mind is restless and needs something to grab onto so having the facilitator sing or whisper Baba Nam Kevalam throughout the meditation can assure a more successful experience for the young child. The child's mind, thoughts, and body are further focused by visual aids (within and/or without) and with kinesthetic experiences through mudras (gestures) or holding something in their hands. Visual, auditory, and kinesthetic involvements are blended with feeling the love, feeling the light, and feeling the goodness.

MEDITATION METHODOLOGY
PREPARATIONS FOR MEDITATION

As a preparation for meditation, singing, chanting, and yogic breathing can bring the unity of spirit and quieting of the mind and body. Inviting children in conversations about "What makes you happy?" or "Who loves you?" can be helpful in bringing positive feelings to their mind, heart, and body which is key to yoga meditation. The facilitator may want to guide this discussion towards things that Mommy, Daddy, or friends do to make us happy rather than physical objects. The children can hold these feelings in their hearts with their hands over their chests during meditation.

The meditation experience has to be both child directed and teacher directed. Children participate more readily when they are involved and given some responsibility concerning the experience. Think about ways to give children choices so that they may participate in a more dynamic way. Daily chose one or two "Lead Children for the Day" to decide what hand position or mudra shall the group express today. How many times will the chant be repeated? Will the children sit or lie down? If seated, will the eyes be open or gazing at an object? If open, from the facilitator's plate of nature objects, which one will be the focus of the day-sitting in the middle of the circle?

MEDITATION POSITIONS

Meditation is practiced in a position comfortably held. For the very young child meditation is sometimes more effective in a lying down position which minimizes distractions. Young children are naturally conditioned to being relaxed when prone. In the Shavasana position they can actually hold their meditation for much longer than when seated. However, seated meditation is also beneficial of course.

MEDITATION TECHNIQUES

Nature objects - Giving each child a nature object to hold. Student may hold a shell, a stone, a pine cone, fairy or dragon tear.

Story meditation – Compose a very short story children hear

while meditating. The children may sit or lie down silently while the facilitator gently sings or chants *Baba Nam Kevalam*.

Bell – The bell guides our way to our inner home within the heart. Softly ring the bell throughout the meditation. Allow it to resonate OR ring it once at the beginning and once at the end. Have a child help you in ringing the bell.

Candle Gazing – Chant together, "I am a child of light. I bring light to every one" and gaze at a candle. Notice the blue at the bottom of the flame – the brown in the middle of the flame. Can you see the wick? Look at the bright yellow part of the flame. It is warm. Repeat, "I am a child of light. I bring light to every one."

Dragon Smiles - Each child may be holding and rubbing a glass dragon tear in one hand. Every time you rub a dragon tear with your finger, a dragon somewhere in the world smiles. (Smooth polished stones also works for this. What other happy things can happen in the world every time you rub the magic stone?)

Little Light of Mine - Invite all the children to tap lightly on their hearts and to look down at their hearts. "Tough the Light. Smile to your Light. Feel your Light. It is always shining deep in your heart even in the night." "Listen listen listen to my light. It shines in my heart even in the night." You can speak to your Light. "Hello Little Light are you there? Hello Little Light are you there?"

Rainbow - Paint a picture in your mind with your eyes closed of the rainbow. Pick one color and cover your whole body in that color. Paint your body from your head to your toes in that color. How does it feel? Isn't this wonderful? It's a color shower.

Flower - Get a rose or other flower. You may get one that will be passed and shared in the class OR you may give one flower to every child. Each one of you is like this flower – beautiful and handsome. You smell wonderful. Everyone is coming to see you, to be near you. Everyone loves you and wants to play with you. Everyone wants you to be their friend.

Singing Bowl - Invite the sound of the bell. Listen, listen, listen to your heart's song.

MEDITATION FLOW

The length of the meditation may be very, very short in the beginning and as the children become more comfortable the time can be lengthened. It should end when they get too wiggly. For 3-5 year olds, four minutes can be a very long time in a group setting.

There are techniques that the facilitator can implement to extend the meditation experience. The facilitator may bring an item and place it on each child's jeart while they are lying down. (They will wait for you to come." "When I see that you are being still, I will place a small animal (or nature object for example) on your heart. You may touch the animal, but please keep your eyes closed. Please stay still." The facilitator will sing Baba Nam Kevalam for a few minutes while placing an object on each heart.

When closing the meditation, consider a sweet song and a collective action that is performed together or individually such as blowing out a candle, holding hands, etc. to conclude this activity and bring unity of purpose and loving to the group.

BENEFITS OF SUSTAINED MEDITATION

There are countless clinical studies on the benefits of meditation. For young children it gives them the opportunity to enjoy the experience of stillness and calmness. It can also encourage the development of concentration, determination, and patience. Meditation engages the brain in many ways, including self-regulation. Such a practice, overtime, brings mental contentment. Psychological and emotional benefits include the stimulation of imagination, memory encoding, lessening of mental storage and retrieval problems, and balancing the emotions.

DOMAIN 8: SAMADHI OR SELF ACTUALIZATION

Samadhi is the result of practicing all of the other domains of Astaunga Yoga. It is the perfect state of equilibrium derived from the daily determined investment of heart, mind, and body in the performance of spiritual yoga practices. The benefits of Samadhi are profound, long lasting contentment, and an actual experience of the Infinite.

In the classroom any steps of contentment, love, relaxation are building blocks for Samadhi. It is the result of all the positive effort in Astaunga Yoga. To help more clearly focus the children towards Samadhi, Neohumanism is indispensable. Neohumanism draws upon the extending of love, affection, and reverence not only to every human being but to all living beings. This is natural for children. Neohumanism redefines every step of education to emphasize this. Every realm of life is engaged in it. In the world of yoga the concept of living or being alive is not exclusively designated only to those that breathe, but includes all life (animate and inanimate) - the air, the minerals, the dirt, plants and trees, insects, beings of the air, all who walk or slither or hop on the earth, as well as those who swim and thrive in the seas. Like indigenous cultures throughout the world, neo-humanism emphasizes how humans share kinship with all created beings of our global family and must live in a way that demonstrates this. Every yogi strives to not intentionally harm any living being and embraces each member of the creation with benevolence. All entities are perceived as expressions of the Divine ~ the One in the Many and the Many in the One.

In meditation, children and teachers can extend their most precious treasure of unconditional love towards everyone. The children are in a collective flow like an ocean wave, moving with all living beings together in harmony. Remind children in their meditations they are love, love is all around them. Everywhere is love. They will get glimpses of samadhi, profound universal love.

By incorporating all the steps of Astaunga yoga, children catch the aim in life is to increasingly love and care more for themselves, for those around them, and for every being. Its daily practice gives deeper meaning to and makes sacred the education process. Children's group effort to perform Astaunga yoga accelerates every individual. They become Beings of Light to each other and find their own brilliance shining brightly inside themselves.

BIBLIOGRAPHY

P.R. Sarkar, "Some Hints on Education," Central Newsletter (August 1980), Calcutta, Ananda Marga Publications, 1980

P.R. Sarkar, *Discourses on Neohumanist Education*, Calcutta, Ananda Marga Publications, 1998

P.R. Sarkar, *Prout in a Nutshell Part 1*, Calcutta, Ananda Marga Publications 1987

P.R. Sarkar, *Prout in a Nutshell Part 18*, Calcutta, Ananda Marga Publications 1987

P.R. Sarkar, "The Practice of Art and Literature", *A Few Problems Solved*, Calcutta, Ananda Marga Publications, 1984

P.R. Sarkar, *Human Society Part 1*, Calcutta, Ananda Marga Publications 1984

P.R. Sarkar, *Problem of the Day*, Calcutta, Ananda Marga Publications 1959

P.R. Sarkar, *Yoga Psychology*, Calcutta, Ananda Marga Publications

P.R. Sarkar, *Thoughts of P.R. Sarkar*, Calcutta, Ananda Marga Publications, 1985

P.R. Sarkar, *Baba's Grace*, California, Ananda Marga Publications, 1973

P.R. Sarkar, *Ananda Vanii*, Anandanagar, India, Ananda Marga Publications, 1978

P.R. Sarkar, Translation of Prabhat Samgiit Song No. 1190, Prabhat Samgiit, Calcutta, Ananda

Shrii Shrii Anandamurti, *Subhasita Samgraha Part 1*, Calcutta, Ananda Marga Publications, 1981

Acarya Prasiidananda Avadhuta, *Neo-Humanism Ecology*, Manila, Ananda Marga Publications, 1990

Vistara Parhem, *What's Wrong with Eating Meat*, USA, Ananda Marga Publications, 1997

P.R. Sarkar, *The Liberation of Intellect – Neo-humanism*, Calcutta, Ananda Marga Publications, 1982

Swami Vivekananda (1863-1902), *Education*, Calcutta, Vedanta Press

Jack Canfield and Mark Victor Hansen, *A 2nd Helping of Chicken Soup for the Soul*, Florida, Health Communications Inc., 1995

Stephan R. Kellar and Alan R. Felthous, "Childhood Cruelty toward Animals among Criminals and Non-Criminals," *Human Relations*, Volume 38, No. 12, USA

Richard J. Barnet, *The Lean Years: Politics in the Age of Scarcity*, New York, Simon And Schuster, 1980

"Teaching Tolerance Project", *Starting Small, Alabama*, Southern Poverty Law Center, 1991

Didi A. Nivedita & Ketana J. Bardwell, *Who Am I?*, Australia, Ananda Marga Publications, 1996

Feeney, Stephanie, Christensen, Doris, Moravcik, Eva, *Who Am I in the Lives of Children?*, Ohio, Merill Publishing Company, 1987

Terry Salinger, *Language Arts and Literacy for Young Children*, New York, Macmillan Publishing Company, 1988

Sarah Ban Breathnach, *Simple Abundance*, New York, Time Warner Company, 1995

About the Author

Nancy "Niiti" Gannon has twenty-four years of experience in early childhood education. She opened and directed preschools in the Philippines, Malaysia, and Guam. Her first educational publication was *For Universal Minds*. This was followed by three teachers' guidebooks: *Safe and Sound*, *Who Am I*, and *I Can Draw the Sun*, co-authored by Ketana Bardwell. She also authored a book on yoga psychology, *Head in the Stars, Feet on the Ground*, and an autobiography, *Meetings With My Master*.

NOTES

1. P.R. Sarkar, "Some Hints on Education," *Central Newsletter (August 1980)*, Calcutta, Ananda Marga Publications, 1980, 37
2. Acarya Prasiidananda Avadhuta, Neo-Humanism Ecology, Manila, Ananda Marga Publications, 1990, 39
3. Vistara Parhem, *What's Wrong with Eating Meat*, USA, Ananda Marga Publications, 19797, 41
4. P.R. Sarkar, *The Liberation of Intellect – Neo-humanism*, Calcutta, Ananda Marga Publications, 1982, 2
5. Ibid, 3-4
6. Sarah Ban Breathnach, *Simple Abundance*, New York, Time Warner Company, 1995
7. P.R. Sarkar, *Human Society Part 1*, Calcutta, Ananda Marga Publications 1984, 56
8. P.R. Sarkar, *Prout in a Nutshell Part 1*, Calcutta, Ananda Marga Publications 1987, 14
9. Swami Vivekananda (1863-1902), *Education*, Calcutta, Vedanta Press
10. P.R. Sarkar, *Human Society Part 1*, Calcutta, Ananda Marga Publications, 1984
11. Ibid
12. P.R. Sarkar, *Yoga Psychology*, Calcutta, Ananda Marga Publications, 6
13. P.R. Sarkar, *Discourses on Neohumanist Education*, Calcutta, Ananda Marga Publications, 1998, 111
14. P.R. Sarkar, *Thoughts of P.R. Sarkar*, Calcutta, Ananda Marga Publications, 1985, 27
15. Ibid, 19-20
16. P.R. Sarkar, *Baba's Grace*, California, Ananda Marga Publications, 1973, 51
17. P.R. Sarkar, *Ananda Vanii*, Anandanagar, India, Ananda Marga Publications, 1978
18. Shrii Shrii Anandamurti, *Subhasita Samgraha Part 1*, Calcutta, Ananda Marga Publications, 1981, 141
19. Sarah Ban Breathnach, *Simple Abundance*, New York, Time Warner Company, 1995
20. Jack Canfield and Mark Victor Hansen, *A 2nd Helping of Chicken Soup for the Soul*, Florida, Health Communications Inc., 1995, 84-85
21. Stephan R. Kellar and Alan R. Felthous, "Childhood Cruelty toward Animals among Criminals and Non-Criminals," *Human Relations, Volume 38, No. 12*, USA, 113-120

22. Richard J. Barnet, *The Lean Years: Politics in the Age of Scarcity*, New York, Simon And Schuster, 1980, 315-516
23. Ibid, 315-316
24. P.R. Sarkar, Translation of Prabhat Samgiit Song No. 1190, *Prabhat Samgiit*, Calcutta, Ananda Marga Publications
25. "Teaching Tolerance Project", *Starting Small*, Alabama, Southern Poverty Law Center, 1991, 16-17
26. Ibid, 16-17
27. P.R. Sarkar, *Prout in a Nutshell Part 18*, Calcutta, Ananda Marga Publications 1987, 44
28. Didi A. Nivedita & Ketana J. Bardwell, *Who Am I?*, Australia, Ananda Marga Publications, 1996, 31-34
29. P.R. Sarkar, *Human Society Part 1*, Calcutta, Ananda Marga Publications 1984, 1
30. P.R. Sarkar, *Yoga Psychology*, Calcutta, Ananda Marga Publications, 123
31. P.R. Sarkar, *Human Society Part 1*, Calcutta, Ananda Marga Publications 1984, 10
32. P.R. Sarkar, *Problem of the Day*, Calcutta, Ananda Marga Publications 1959, 36
33. Feeney, Stephanie, Christensen, Doris, Moravcik, Eva, *Who Am I in the Lives of Children?*, Ohio, Merill Publishing Company, 1987, 88-91
34. P.R. Sarkar, *Thoughts of P.R. Sarkar*, Calcutta, Ananda Marga Publications, 1985, 171
35. "Teaching Tolerance Project", *Starting Small*, Alabama, Southern Poverty Law Center, 1991
36. Albert Einstein (renown physicist commented on education when asked why after his final exams he did not do any science work.)
37. Swami Vivekananda (1863-1902), *Education,* Calcutta, Vedanta Press
38. P.R. Sarkar, *Prout in a Nutshell Part 18*, Calcutta, Ananda Marga Publications 1987, 17
39. Jack Canfield and Mark Victor Hansen, *A 2nd Helping of Chicken Soup for the Soul*, Florida, Health Communications Inc., 1995, 86
40. P.R. Sarkar, *Human Society Part 1*, Calcutta, Ananda Marga Publications 1984, 45
41. P.R. Sarkar, "Some Hints on Education," *Central Newsletter (August 1980)*, Calcutta, Ananda Marga Publications, 1980, 37
42. Didi A. Nivedita & Ketana J. Bardwell, *Who Am I?*, Australia, Ananda Marga Publications, 1996, 42
43. P.R. Sarkar, "Some Hints on Education," *Central Newsletter (August 1980)*, Calcutta, Ananda Marga Publications, 1980, 37
44. Sarah Ban Breathnach, *Simple Abundance*, New York, Time Warner Company, 1995

45. Terry Salinger, *Language Arts and Literacy for Young Children*, New York, Macmillan Publishing Company, 1988, 4
46. P.R. Sarkar, *Discourses on Neohumanist Education*, Calcutta, Ananda Marga Publications, 1998, 124
47. Sarah Ban Breathnach, *Simple Abundance*, New York, Time Warner Company, 1995
48. P.R. Sarkar, "The Practice of Art and Literature", *A Few Problems Solved*, Calcutta, Ananda Marga Publications, 1984
49. P.R. Sarkar, *Prout in a Nutshell Part 18*, Calcutta, Ananda Marga Publications 1987, 17
50. Sarah Ban Breathnach, *Simple Abundance*, New York, Time Warner Company, 1995
51. Sarah Ban Breathnach, *Simple Abundance*, New York, Time Warner Company, 1995
52. Sarah Ban Breathnach, *Simple Abundance*, New York, Time Warner Company, 1995
53. Sarah Ban Breathnach, *Simple Abundance*, New York, Time Warner Company, 1995
54. Vistara Parhem, *What's Wrong with Eating Meat*, USA, Ananda Marga Publications, 19797, 38-39
55. Sarah Ban Breathnach, *Simple Abundance*, New York, Time Warner Company, 1995
56. P.R. Sarkar, *Thoughts of P.R. Sarkar*, Calcutta, Ananda Marga Publications, 1985, 63
57. P.R. Sarkar, *The Liberation of Intellect – Neo-humanism*, Calcutta, Ananda Marga Publications, 1982, 101
58. Ibid, 10
59. P.R. Sarkar, *Discourses on Neohumanist Education*, Calcutta, Ananda Marga Publications, 1998, 111

www.ingramcontent.com/pod-product-compliance
Lightning Source LLC
Chambersburg PA
CBHW021107080526
44587CB00010B/424